Secrets OF AN Irresistible Woman

Michelle McKINNEY HAMMOND

HARVEST HOUSE PUBLISHER
Eugene, Oregon 97402

Cover by Koechel Peterson and Associates, Minneapolis, Minnesota.

SECRETS OF AN IRRESISTIBLE WOMAN

Copyright © 1998 by Michelle McKinney-Hammond
Published by Harvest House Publishers.
Eugene, Oregon 97402

Library of Congress Cataloging-in-Publication Data

McKinney-Hammond, Michelle, 1957-
    Secrets of an irresistible woman / Michelle McKinney-Hammond.
        p.   cm.
    ISBN 1-56507-843-8
    1. Mate selection. 2. Man-woman relationships. 3. Women—Conduct
of life. I. Title.
HQ801.M4879 1998
646.7'7—DC21   97-29011
                                                                   CIP

Printed in the United States of America.

.   05 06 07 08 09 / BC / 20 19 18 17

To God, my Heavenly Father,
who lovingly designed all of the "rules" for my own good.

To my parents who followed suit:
George and Charity Hammond and
William and Norma McKinney

To my uncles and aunts who, to me, personified the rules:
Stanley and Eglantine White
Kow and Marion Aarkah
Ernesta Branker
What wonderful examples you have been to me!

To my pastor's wife, Wanda Eckhardt
a truly "Irresistible Woman."
I'm watching, learning, and taking notes!

To two of the most special young ladies I know:
Elsie and Nicole Duncan-Williams
You'll always be my girls,
and you're never too young to learn the rules.

Acknowledgments

To my sisters Nicole, Ayodele, Annette, Jacqueline, Karen, Yaaba, Anna, Myma, and Ama—perhaps if we stick together we can master this thing called "being a woman of God." (smile)

To my sisters in Christ, too many to name, but some have louder voices than others (listed in alphabetical order, not in order of importance)—Cindy Bastounes, Brenda Blonski, Charlot Fortier, Sheila Frazier, Lydia Garlington, Theresa Hayden, Charlotte Kroot, Karen McDonald, Terri McFadden, Alda Denise Mitchell, Nancy Roberts, Dorothy Ross, Sylvia Sausedo, Susan Sharpe, Jan Shurtz, Michelle Taylor, Sunday Williams, Theresa Williams, Lorraine Williamson, and Philomina "Bunny" Wilson. Hey ladies, thanks for "getting in my Kool-aid" and holding me accountable! Couldn't do it without you.

To the entire Harvest House family—your enthusiasm is contagious and motivating. Thank you for all of your support; it has been truly nurturing.

Contents

Introduction

Recently a book titled *The Rules* hit the bookstands and seemed to set the singles community on its ear. As the book's two female authors made the talk show circuit, I sat eyebrows to scalp, quite intrigued by the effect this simple little book was having on men and women alike. I mean people were downright upset about *The Rules*! Those who had applied the book's suggestions reported their success while the audience looked on in disgust. The authors themselves seemed befuddled by the insults that were hurled their way by the audience, although I'm sure they laughed all the way to the bank afterwards. After all, in spite of people's adverse reactions the book was a bestseller.

After a bit of thought, I realized why so many people were upset by *The Rules'* suggestions. Most women today had too much free time on their hands, and lacked the self-esteem to be able to put into practice what the authors advised. It was as if the Ten Commandments had been introduced all over again. Women were overwhelmed by their own inability to live up to what seemed to be difficult standards. I felt as if everyone had missed the real point of the book, including the authors, who seemed to have a difficult time defending their material other than to respond, "Well, if you want to get married..." The point to me was very simple—they were basically saying, "Get a life!" If a woman had a life, she would automatically do all the things that were suggested in the book.

And why were the men upset? As one well-known talk show hostess concluded, "I believe men like women who conduct themselves in this way; they just don't want to know they're following an instruction manual." I was inclined to agree.

After *The Rules* was released, many people felt compelled to write their own version of the book or respond to what these women had written, including myself. I felt that their premise for writing the book was well-founded. When it came to dating, mating, and relating no one seemed to know what to do anymore. The relationship game had become a free-for-all, with everyone playing it by ear. The results were generally miserable, but no one knew what else to do so they continued playing the same game and blaming any failure on the other person. I believe the entire problem boils down to one simple observation: Women, in their desperation to have someone in their lives, have forfeited their power and have become frustrated victims in affairs of the heart.

A friend of mine once said, "God gave men testosterone so that they would make a commitment." But, sadly, many women have short-circuited the commitment process by violating all the safeguards God gave them to heighten their desirability and get them happily married. No longer are women considered *trés cher*, as the French would say. *Cher* means "expensive" in French; the same word also means "dear." Instead of realizing their own worth, many women today have put themselves on sale, lowering their value along with their standards, settling for less than the best for themselves. More often than not, they have embraced the philosophy that anything is better than nothing. This is what happens when a woman has no idea where she is going or what she is entitled to. As the Word says, "My people are destroyed for lack of knowledge. Because you have rejected knowledge, I also will reject you" (Hosea 4:6 NKJV). That's deep but true—a lack of knowledge will cause us to lose or suffer rejection every time, in every area of our lives.

I realize this relationship thing is more than just a notion, but it was designed to be a whole lot simpler than we've made it. I've bumped around out here for a long time myself and made all the classic mistakes. Fortunately, I've lived and learned, which is something that could benefit all of us. Don't you think it's time you got it together, too? Your head is too pretty to keep banging it against a wall.

So now is the time to throw out all that self-destructive behavior, and get on with becoming women fully prepared to be blessed with mates who are deserving of our hand. So pull up a chair and let's really talk, girlfriend. I am here to dish up the real lowdown on how this thing called the pursuit of love should go. This is the real nitty-gritty the way God serves it up. That's right, the spiritual 4-1-1 on this romance business for your consideration, and hopefully your consumption. So read, absorb, and practice…oh, and when Mr. Man does show up, keep your head, keep the rules, and reap the benefits.

1

All Rules
Are Made to Be Broken?
I Don't Think So, Girlfriend!

All right, already, so you've heard all "the rules" before, you say. Girls don't call boys, don't buy them presents, play hard to get, and so on and so on.... Your mother crammed them into your head as you headed out the door to high school. You thought they were old-fashioned then, and you most certainly think they are antiquated now. After all, this is the nineties, isn't it? Well, you won't get an "amen" out of me. By breaking my share of the rules and suffering the miserable consequences that follow, I've finally come to the conclusion that mama just might have been on to something.

"Say it ain't so!" you cry. But my answer back to you is, "'Tis too." And this is based on research, not on what Oprah had to say, okay? After rolling around what works and what doesn't with all of my friends, I decided to take up this discussion with The Man. You know, The Main Man—God. I figured if anybody knew how this male-female thing was supposed to work, He did. He in turn assured me that all the answers I was seeking could be found in His Word, and with a little prayer, some diligent study, and a healthy dose of His wisdom, I would be able to figure out His perfect design for this relationship mystery once and for all.

Once I got into it, I must admit I "oohed" and "aahed" a lot. Suddenly the light went on! I had made a lot of mistakes in the name of my own personality. Mmm hmm, I know you know what I'm talking about because you've said it too whenever someone said you needed to change your approach with a man. "Well, this is just the way I am. Anybody who doesn't like it can take a hike!" And so they have. Let's face it, if you live in a house that's falling down around your ears and no one wants to visit you, why sit there and complain about everyone's lack of understanding? Obviously, it's time to move to a new address that others feel comfortable visiting.

Self-justification in the face of harmful habits can be the absolute worst deceiver and robber of our happiness. In a society that spends much of its time looking for others to blame, the concept of needful change is often overlooked. But I present the idea of change to you from another perspective. Let's look at change as growth, which is what all spiritually-minded women should do. Actually, this is something that all smart and effective people tend to do. And the Bible certainly backs me up on this one. Proverbs 12:15 says, "The way of a fool seems right to him, but a wise man listens to advice (NIV). This could also be rendered, "A fool despises correction."

Let's think about it from another perspective. When any major business sees its profit margin not moving or even declining, management's first move often is to call in a consultant. This consultant goes over the company's business plan and all steps taken up to the present with a fine-tooth comb. Then the consultant evaluates the entire operation, locates problem spots, and maps out where the company needs to revamp or change its approach in order to expand and *grow*. (There's that word again!)

"But this isn't a business, this is my heart you're talking about," you protest. Yes, I know that. You didn't think I could be spiritual without discernment, did you? Bear with me, we're discussing *principles* here. I want you to grasp the idea of change being growth. It's funny that most people aren't opposed to a nose job here, or a little nip and tuck there. So what's all the fuss about getting a facelift on the *inside*? It's less expensive, I'll tell you that. And no, this is not about being deceitful, pretending to be someone you're not, playing games, or being manipulative. As you know, these things violate the law of the Spirit.

So based on several scriptural lessons—as well as my own personal experiences and what women by and large are saying—I think it's time to revisit this whole *rules* thing, minus the hype, and get some understanding.

Are *The Rules* made to be broken? Let me put it this way: When God made the Ten Commandments He didn't call them the Ten Suggestions. He meant what He said and had a good reason for each one of them. Even though you are free to do as you like, you need to know that the laws of the Spirit are a permanent mandate. So for every broken *Rule*, even though God's love and forgiveness are always available, there will still be an unhappy consequence. And if you're honest with yourself, you'll admit the negative consequence far overshadows the joy of whatever little self-indulgence you dipped your fingers into.

Now don't tell my mother this, but since I've started following *The Rules* I've been a much happier person. This really odd thing happened to me—my self-esteem zoomed way up. I found myself mimicking Sally Field at the Oscars crying in jubilance, "You like me, you really like me!" Why? Because I had finally given myself the chance to find out that I was a lovable woman simply because I was *me*! Actually, you *can* go ahead and tell my mother because I found out they're not really my mother's rules. They're God's rules, created to make me feel like the special woman He designed me to be.

On that note, I hope that by the time I finish pulling your coattail about how *The Rules* might not be "politically correct" but are actually quite "spiritually correct," perhaps you, too, will have a change of heart.

Prayer

Heavenly Father, I now submit my spirit, my heart, and my mind to You. Take them and transform them into the original image of the woman You created me to be. Guide me and renew me by the transforming power of Your word. Grant me insight into Your design for love and marriage. Forgive my stubbornness in the areas of self-defeating habits. Expose every blind spot and every area of denial in my heart. Help me to obey Your principles and break the chains over my life that keep me from having fruitful relationships. Free me to give and receive love as never before, in Jesus' Name. Amen.

2

So Who Wrote
The Rules Anyway?

*J*ust in case you're wondering why rules are needed in the first place, let me break it down to you plain and simple: Rules are needed to maintain order. Imagine a world filled with all chiefs and no Indians. Imagine a busy street with no lanes marked, no stoplights, and no crosswalks. Can you imagine the chaos that would result? Just think about the turmoil that happens now every time someone ignores a yield sign or a stoplight, and multiply that ad infinitum. I can vouch for what a mess it would be because I've been the unfortunate victim of a disobedient driver. People get hurt when people break the rules!

We all need to set boundaries in order to peacefully coexist. Something as simple as staying to the right when you walk down a crowded sidewalk makes the journey a whole lot smoother than if you choose to cross over to the left and walk against the flow of traffic. Suddenly you find yourself weaving in and out of people and saying "excuse me" a thousand times, sometimes in the face of some pretty irate expressions. Why? Because by walking on the wrong side, you are disturbing the natural flow and order of things. From relationships to the flow of traffic, the principle remains the same: Stay in order and things will move smoothly; get out of order and you will run smack-dab into difficulty or, even worse, disaster.

Women who are walking in the Spirit understand that they serve a mighty King. Though they are in this world, they are certainly not of it; their real citizenship belongs to a higher kingdom where order rules. Our God is a God of order. His rules are good rules, made for the benefit of His people, even in the area of courtship. If you look back to the days of gallant knights and royal ladies, people practiced something called "protocol" when it came to affairs of the heart. Everyone knew what to expect and which roles were played by whom. Well, we've gotten away from that protocol in the name of today's so-called liberation. But what I'm still trying to figure out is exactly who got liberated. One look around at the state of most relationships and the lives of those walking solo in search of the perfect mate tells me that all liberation accomplished was to lead most of us into emotional bondage. It makes me think of the song "Three Blind Mice." Have you ever seen such a confused group of people in your life? The women are angry, and the men are scratching their heads and asking, "What did I do?" Let's hear it for liberation. Did I hear a low-key "whoopee"?

So we ask ourselves, *can certain rules really make or break a relationship? And just who is the final authority on all of these rules, anyway?* God is! He was the first one on the scene, and therefore He earned the right to write the book on love and relationships since He created them. And thank goodness for that! The Bible says, "There is a way that seems right to a man, but in the end it leads to death [or destruction]" (Proverbs 14:12 NIV). So much for our human opinion. Let's face it, we are fickle people. Just look at our society. Last year's taboo has become this year's alternative lifestyle.

So who gets to regulate the meter on right or wrong in the midst of an ever-changing society? Which man or woman could be trusted to stand constant amid the shifting tides of ever-evolving values? God is the only one who qualifies. The only one objective enough not to take sides or be manipulated by the reasonings of the masses or the cries of special interest groups.

That brings us to the discovery that God's rules for relationships not only are not suggestions, but essential laws, with serious consequences when they're broken. They were written knowing what is best for us. Yes, God actually does take our feelings into consideration when coming up with these rules. He's not some stuffy old man sitting on a throne trying to think up ways to ruin our lives and spoil our fun. His rules are a wonderful part of the proof of His love for you and me. He loved us so much that He sat down and figured out the best way to protect our hearts—and that is what His rules are really all about.

When God made woman He also designed how He wanted her to be treated. Very carefully. Like a precious glass sculpture. It was never his intention for women's hearts to be jostled around the way they have been. He created us to be protected, loved, and cared for. But when sin entered the world it was like a virus had been injected into the computer program that controls our hearts. Ever since then, the messages between men and women have been scrambled and we've had trouble deciphering the code.

"It's hard being a woman," you may say. And I believe it is if you're trying to be someone other than who you were created to be. If you are trying to take on the role of a man, then you're absolutely headed for trouble. The difficulty comes from forcing yourself to fit into a space you were not designed to fill.

Now before you get upset with me, know that I'm not talking about any specific theme on rights. What I'm talking about is our basic makeup, how we were constructed—spiritually, emotionally, and physically. Our role the way God designed it, is for our own protection. He did not create us as inferior beings or as doormats for men to walk on or take advantage of. But if we take a good look at most present-day relationships, we've certainly done a fine job of putting ourselves in these positions. The only way that any woman can honestly say and believe that a man has held her down or set her back is if she hasn't gotten a true understanding of her own power as a woman. Remember, it was a woman who influenced a man to sin in the first place. We, as women, wield the scepter of influence for good or evil in a man's life. Adam forfeited a perfect existence in order to remain by Eve's side. Now that's what I call power!

Keeping that in mind, you can be encouraged that God's rules were designed to save us from the consequences of the painful choices we feel inclined to make. It's important to understand His motivation. It's always been easier to take advice from someone who you believe loves you. Well guess what, honey? God loves you! He wants the man in your life to be the physical manifestation of His love for you. And He is so serious about this that he wrote in His Word, "In the same way, you married men should live considerately with your wives, with an intelligent recognition of the marriage relation, honoring the woman as the physically weaker partner, but realizing that you are joint heirs of the grace (God's unmerited favor) of life, in order that your prayers may not be hindered and cut off" (1 Peter 3:7 AMP).

Imagine that! God watches over His women so jealously, He warns man that his mistreatment of women will lead to ineffective prayer. Mr. Husband's ability to get a request through to God is based on his treatment of you! Are you feeling important, powerful, and special yet? You should be!

Don't worry if you're not yet convinced. I think you will be by the time you finish reading more about God's rules. And by the way, I think it's time to give *The Rules* a new name. Because we are all spiritual women, I am no longer going to refer to *The Rules* as the rules. I've decided to rename them *The Principles*.

I know that all spiritually inclined women are able to receive the wisdom of spiritual truths and recognize them as valuable instruments in our spiritual and physical hands. Therefore I'm confident that we shall serenely proceed through this journey to discovering love as God intended it. We will not bash men or dabble in self-abasement. Instead, we will accept that no one is perfect, get over our past disappointments, and get on with the exciting journey. After all, "…all have sinned and fall short of the glory of God" (Romans 3:23). In short, people make mistakes—and more often than not, I've found it has little or next to nothing to do with us and everything to do with them and their own personal issues. So let's not nurse and rehearse the last sad song; let's stop licking our wounds, submit them to God, get healed, and proceed on to victory.

Well, are you ready? I sure am! But before we take a look at anyone else, let's take a good look at ourselves.

Prayer

Heavenly Father, I ask that You grant me the gift of Your divine perspective on affairs of the heart. Help me to grasp the revelation of Your design for my life. Give me a willingness to trust You with my heart as I choose to do things Your way. Help me not to settle for the world's deception, but to grasp Your truth with confidence. Give me the strength to depend on the move of Your Spirit over the devices and manipulations of the flesh. Teach me, Lord. I surrender all of my preconceived notions and baggage from the past. I give You my heart and ask that You help me to begin again on Your terms, in Jesus' Name. Amen.

3

A Woman of
Spiritual Principle

*B*ack in the seventies the Isley Brothers sang a song called "Who's That Lady." Those words have passed across the lips of countless men throughout history as some woman ever-so-confidently floated through a room without so much as a backward glance at them. Only those observing her from a safe corner were able to see the entire picture unfold. This woman worked these men's nerves quietly without ever noticing, as she sipped her punch or spoke with her friends, that the rest of the room was up for grabs. I recognize that woman. I have seen her at work before. She is a woman of spiritual principle—a *Principles* woman.

Who exactly is a *Principles* woman? Well, not only does she have a learned knowledge of who she is and how she should be treated, she also has an *understanding*. Have you ever known people who have lots of *knowledge* but they don't seem to truly understand things? I thought so! This *Principles* woman knows what time it is, and she understands exactly what she deserves. This girl has wrapped the girdle of truth around her tightly and there is nothing flabby about her program! But we'll talk more about that later.

A *Principles* Woman

The sum total of the deal is this: a *Principles* woman knows who she is in the eyes of God and understands her worth. She is firmly committed to not living beneath her privilege. She sees herself "seated in heavenly places" (see Ephesians 2:6) with a rich inheritance. We are talking royalty here! She will not allow herself to be mishandled by someone who is a spiritual and emotional pauper. Her position isn't something she boldly proclaims, but everything about her actions and the way she carries herself says it, if you get my drift. This woman understands "Who can find a virtuous woman? for her price is far above rubies" (Proverbs 31:10 KJV). A *Principles* woman knows that she is a valuable jewel and that the right discerning eye will see her worth and act accordingly. Nothing but an equally precious setting will do for her!

A *Principles* woman is not only a woman of unsurpassable character, she's "got it going on" in every way. Her head is together, her heart is together, her spirit is together, and she has developed and is actively using her gifts. She is a person who draws others to her because she has something that everyone wants—she has a certain "joie de vivre," a joy of life that comes from being comfortable with who she is.

Let me ask you something: if you met yourself walking down the street would you want to be your friend? If the answer to this question is *no*, you've got some work to do, but not to worry! By the time you finish this book, you'll be overflowing with self-appreciation, and you'll also be more appreciative of those other people called men. Yes, they really are people too. A little strange but, hey!

A *Principles* woman knows the promises of God concerning her and keeps them close to her heart. She won't settle for less than God's best for herself. After all, that's what He's promised, and "Blessed is she that believed: for there shall be a performance of those things which were told her from the Lord" (Luke 1:45 KJV). And when people know you expect the very best, guess what—they give it!

A *Principles* woman is a well-kept lady. She keeps herself reserved for those things that are deserving of her attention. She doesn't get distracted by or caught up in things that are not edifying or uplifting to herself or to those in her world. She keeps her affections closely guarded and never freely tosses them to the wind in the hopes that someone will catch them. She understands that she must, "Keep your heart with all diligence, for out of it spring the issues of life" (Proverbs 4:23 NKJV). Or, in the words of another translation, "Above all else, guard your heart, for it affects everything you do." Her life demands respect from all who know her.

A first class pilot, a *Principles* woman soars above negativity and other people's trivial opinions. She knows where she's going and what she wants, and she doesn't land until she sees her destination and gets clearance from God. She understands and knows that when she decides to rise above the negativity in her life, she'll find the crowd thinning the higher she goes. Not to worry! There may be fewer people, but they're a whole lot nicer. Plus, a *Principles* woman is quite comfortable flying solo; she knows that she's never really alone. She only wants a rightly qualified copilot to fill the seat beside her.

A *Principles* Woman in Action

And last, but not least, a *Principles* woman is a lady at all times. Keeping this standard takes some work—and the grace of God in some circumstances, believe you me! I think I realized the difference between walking in the flesh and walking in the spirit on a recent publicity tour for my previous book, *What to Do Until Love Finds You.* I had flown from Chicago to Toronto on Sunday to tape a Monday morning television show, then returned to the airport to fly back to Chicago and continue on to Tampa, Florida. (Did you follow that?) On top of that, I missed my original flight to Toronto due to a grouchy driver and had to spend an additional two hours at the airport before getting another plane. You can imagine that, after all of this traveling, I was quite exhausted by the time I reached my destination at eleven o'clock that night!

I had visions of falling into bed immediately and waking up refreshed for my two television interviews the next day. Imagine my chagrin upon discovering that my bag had not made the flight! Here I stood in winter clothes and boots, no less, in warm, humid

Florida. I had spilled something down the front of the jacket, and I was quite rumpled beyond repair from my long day of traveling. Needless to say, I was not camera-ready! After confirming that there was no way I could have my bag, which held a beautiful new suit and dress, in time for my interviews the next day, I set off in search of a pharmacy. I needed to purchase some basic essentials— a toothbrush, hair rollers, deodorant, makeup...yes, everything was in my bag!

Outside the airport I hailed a cab and told the cab driver my predicament. We found a pharmacy and strolled down its aisles as a voice on the loudspeaker warned everyone that the store would close in five minutes. I hurriedly collected everything I needed, which was quite a feat since I was in completely unfamiliar territory dealing with products I was not accustomed to. I deposited my selections on the cashier's table only to be told that the pharmacy did not accept out-of-town checks. I didn't have a credit card on me that I could use. Beyond that, I had already taken out my cash station limit for the day, and I was only carrying enough cash to cover my cab fare. *Okay*, I said to myself, *I'll just get the basics and hope the television station has my shade of makeup.*

The cab driver, who had been kind enough to wait for me while I went on my little toiletries expedition, suggested I go to Walmart, where I could write a check and perhaps find an outfit. At this I broke into peals of laughter. Me, shopping for an outfit at Walmart! If my friends could see me now! Now this is not a slam against Walmart, but in light of my dressing habits this was price-less. I just happen to be the diva of Anne Klein, Donna Karan, Ellen Tracy, and Dana Buchman. But, being a *Principles* woman of the creative persuasion, I found a large scarf I could wear as a skirt and a short-sleeved raw silk top. Along with a pair of black fabric sandals and some underwear, I was almost set. Now all I needed was some lotion. When I asked where the skin-care products could be found, I was told that particular section of the store had just had the floor waxed and was roped off. So I took a deep breath and went in search of baby oil. No baby oil. Well, at this point I decided Vaseline would have to do. I was truly down to the basics here!

On that note I set off for the hotel. By now my watch read two A.M. and I was anxious just to finally sit down. I checked in at the hotel and got on the elevator, dragging all of my loot behind me along with my computer. As the elevator door closed, my panty hose promptly lost their elasticity and fell down around my knees. At this point, I didn't even bother to try to pull them back up. I just waddled to my room, purchases in tow, dragging on the floor behind me.

The next morning I breezed into the television station apologizing for scaring them in my au natural state, and asked where I could find the makeup room. Makeup room? There was no makeup room. In addition, there was no makeup! "Okay, can someone take me to the store?" I asked. They were happy to oblige, so off I went, back to my favorite little pharmacy. This time I went directly to the cash station next door to get out money for my purchases. Guess what? The cash station was out of order.

So this *Principles* woman marched into the store, resolving to exercise her spiritual authority. I'd truly had enough of the devil's antics by now, and I was not going to give him the satisfaction of seeing me crack under the pressure. I selected everything I needed, strode to the counter, and confidently informed the cashier I *had* to write an out-of-town check. The tone of my voice must have convinced them I wouldn't take no for an answer! They accepted my check and back to the studio I fled. I now had only five minutes to do my makeup, it was a live broadcast, I was the only guest, and they had started the show without me! Don't ask me what I said once I made my breathless entrance onto the set. The rest is a blur. When I later arrived at the airport to return home, there was my bag waiting to go with me. I think I heard it chuckle at me!

When I told my publisher this story, they were amazed that I could laugh about this experience. But that is what a *Principles* woman does. She keeps her head while everyone else around her is losing theirs. She never goes off, even when tempted to excuse herself from the presence of Jesus. She manages to stifle the urge, and she lets God fight her battles. This is a lot easier on the fingernails, believe you me!

Now if you've become overwhelmed by all the attributes of a *Principles* woman and don't feel like you quite measure up or have it all together, don't fret my pet! Help is on the way. We are going to walk through this together, so get those wings ready, click your heels together and pretend you're Dorothy—except I have something different for you to say:

When I rise
　full of love
　　for life and laughter
　　　and the me that I am
　　love will meet me...
　　　when I rise
　　　　above my own neediness
　　　fears
　　　　and frustrated tears
　　and allow myself to be warmed by the Son
　　　love will shine on me...
　when I rise
　　past prayerlessness
desperate hopes
　　sleepless nights
　　　and wondering why I'm alone
　　　　love will wrap me in its arms...
when I rise
　beyond sacrificing who I am
　　mistreating my heart
　　and giving my affections
　　　too freely to the ungrateful...
　when I rise
　　above
　　　accepting scraps
　　　　when I crave for a whole slice of cake
　　　reaching for carrots
　　　　that are merely mirages of together forever
　　accepting another's rejection
　　　as validation of my undesirability...
　when I rise...
　　oh when I rise
　　　when I rise above it all
　　　　my wings will carry me
　　　　　to a place called faith
　　　　　and deliverance
　　　　a place where
　　　　　the lies whispered in the dark
　　　　　must flee

in the face of such intense light...
for this is the place
where God is
and love dwells
for God and love are the same...
and as I rise ever higher
chains snapping from my heart
my mind
my soul
I soar ever higher
carried on the wings of love itself...
yes I rise
and love kisses me deeply
ever so sweetly
and whispers
I'm home....

Prayer

Dear Lord, take me to the place that is higher than me in You. Take me to the place of resting in You and in who You created me to be. Help me to rise to the occasion of glorifying You in all I say and do. Make me rich with the understanding of what it means to truly be a child of God. Help me to walk the walk and not just talk the talk. Let me be a moving illustration of who You are in a way that blesses all I encounter. Help me to forge a new reputation, not just as a woman, but as a woman of God, rising in the Spirit to each situation I encounter, in Jesus' Name. Amen.

Principle #1

Take Art Appreciation

*D*own through the ages men have carved statues, painted pictures, and written songs in tribute to the beauty of women, yet many women have struggled with having a sense of their own beauty. I, however, think it's high time we began to believe a little bit of our own press.

I'm talking about Art Appreciation 101 here. Look in the mirror and face it. You are a work of art! You may not say so, but God does. When He made you He said, "Oh, this is good!" I suggest you begin by echoing the words of David, "I will praise You, for I am fearfully and wonderfully made; marvelous are Your works, and that my soul knows very well" (Psalms 139:14 NKJV). You better believe it and receive it! You'll find yourself in a much better frame of mind.

You're a Work of Art

Just in case you're having some initial difficulty with this, let's go through this exercise slowly. Go to an art museum and examine every painting and sculpture with women as the subjects. You should really enjoy this if you feel you're overweight because most of the old masters—look at a Renoir—liked women who had "meat on their bones." Find a painting or statue that resembles your own body and study it. Look at the lines, the lighting...beautiful, no? "Sure, but that's a painting and this is me," you say. Now don't start tuning up on that sour note! Look again. What's the difference? Why do you think the painting is beautiful but you're not? It's the same body. Think about it. The painting is merely an image of your reflection on a cold, hard surface. You, on the other hand, are warm, vibrant, breathing, and alive with a whole lot of love to give. Talk about a work of art!

But that is only the beginning of the exercise. Next you should go home and look in the mirror, study each of your features, attach a Scripture to them that makes them beautiful, and personalize it. For instance, if you have a problem with your mouth try this one: "[I] open my mouth with wisdom, and on my tongue is the law of kindness" (see Proverbs 31:26 NKJV). Wisdom and kindness make a person attractive. Keep repeating the verse until it gets from your head to your heart to your spirit, and then watch out! You'll start to look real cute to yourself *and* to others.

The Most Important Beauty Tip

You see, the secret to this whole thing is knowing the source of real beauty. Have you ever seen a fantastic-looking man with a plain-looking woman? If you got a chance to ask him what he finds so attractive about this woman, he'd almost certainly begin to go on and on about how sweet she is and how wonderful she makes him feel. Are you getting this? The real beauty tip is found at the end of a dissertation on a very beautiful woman in Proverbs 31. The writer sums up everything about her in one simple sentence: "Charm and grace are deceptive, and beauty is vain [because it is not lasting], but a woman who reverently and worshipfully fears the Lord, she shall be praised!" (verse 30).

That's where it all begins. As we allow the love of God to change our nature and transform us into the *Principles* women he intended us to be, we blossom into beautiful flowers that others will want to stop and admire. And the beauty of a flower is that it just *is*. It doesn't bend over backwards (unless the wind blows), it doesn't perform, buy gifts, make phone calls, or make the first move. It *is* the gift. It doesn't do anything special to get attention. It just stands tastefully in its place and accepts all looks of admiration gracefully.

Ever notice what happens when a beautiful flower catches the eye of an admirer? He can't resist coming closer to smell its fragrance. This is intimacy at its best. An experience like this inspired King Solomon to tell the Shulamite woman, "The fig tree forms its early fruit; the blossoming vines spread their fragrance. Arise, come, my darling; my beautiful one, come with me" (Song of Songs 2:13 NIV). In other words, "Love is beginning to bloom, I feel it in the air, it smells good to me, and I'd like it to linger; therefore, I'm taking this bunch with me." Now is not the time to push the issue. Just keep looking and smelling good, if you know what I mean. Let him get addicted to your fragrance. There's no need for you to launch a campaign of phone calls, cards, and thoughtful little gifts to convince him he made the right choice by "picking" you. Chill out and sit pretty. Allow yourself the luxury of being appreciated. But you'll only be able to do this if you've passed your art appreciation course!

Accept Compliments Gracefully

I once met a very handsome man at a time in my life when I felt overweight. He kept telling me how beautiful I was but I just could not accept his words. So I proceeded to show him pictures of myself when I was slimmer. And you know what happened? I talked him into agreeing that I was currently overweight! He began asking me, "So, how's your diet going?" And I would reply, "What are you trying to say? Do you think I'm fat or something?" And then of course he would say, "Oh, no, not at all! You said you needed to lose weight, so I was merely encouraging you." In my mind I was thinking, "Sure you were!" Get the picture?

The lesson to be learned? We will remain beautiful in the eye of the beholder until we convince him otherwise. So stifle the urge to point out your flaws that you think have gone unnoticed. Perhaps he noticed them and deemed them cute in a quirky kind of way, or he simply didn't think they were important. Practice accepting compliments with a simple "thank you" whether you believe them or not. It can only work in your favor. After all, what they don't notice won't hurt them (or you). And who knows? Maybe in time your mind will be able to catch up with your Creator's vision and you'll finally discover that you're more than all right. As a matter of fact, you're a *Principles* woman who is downright gorgeous in her own unique way!

So imagine your mirror is a frame and strike a pose. You look mah-velous, dahlink! And the sooner you believe it, the sooner others will too.

Prayer

Dear Heavenly Father, help me to see myself through Your eyes. Let the things You reveal to me move from my head to my heart and take root. I ask that You erase the tape of hurtful words, unedifying thoughts, and negative comments that plays in my spirit, and that You replace it with the truth of Your word that "I am fearfully and wonderfully made." Fill me with the worth I have as a daughter of the King. Help me to walk in this newfound identity with a spirit of grace and godly confidence. Let me be a reflection of Your peace and beauty, in Jesus' Name. Amen.

Stop Playing with Daisies!

"*H*e loves me, he loves me not...he loves me, he loves me not." Puh-leeze, girl-friend. You had better be able to rely on more than a flower petal count in order to know if this man loves you or not! And while you might not have specifically questioned a flower about a guy's love for you since you were in grade school, you've probably had this discourse with yourself or with a friend as you pored over every minute detail of your most recent relationship, looking for some sort of answer.

I'm sure you yourself have been a frustrated witness as one of your friends put up with the shenanigans of some knucklehead she just couldn't shake because the guy kept dangling emotional carrots in front of her face. When you tried to be the voice of reason, your poor pathetic friend looked at you and said, "But he told me he *loved* me." To which you replied, "The way he was treating you didn't look much like love to me!" Funny how much easier it is to spot other people's mistakes in love than our own. But this is where leading a spirit-filled life comes in. *Principles* women know what real love looks like and they settle for nothing less.

The Look of Love

"So," you say, "what does real love look like?" I think it's important to take God's opinion on this one because the response from mere mortals would reap a montage of comments from the deeply philosophical to the absolutely ridiculous. And our friends' opinions are usually derived from the things they've been through. Everyone's had a variety of experiences in this arena, some good, some bad. Whatever the theme of love has been in your life, whatever's been consistent to you is accepted to be "the way things are." But your "normal" might not necessarily be healthy. To the consistently used and misused, abusive treatment might be the only kind of "love" they know. And we all know that is not real love.

It is important for a *Principles* woman to study what love looks like from God's point of view because God has the only perfect revelation of love. When people are being trained to recognize counterfeit dollars they don't study endless samples of counterfeit money. Instead, they examine the real thing for countless hours. The lines, the texture, the color—it's all indelibly burned into their memory banks. Then when they're slipped a fake bill, their internal sensors go off like bank alarms because the real thing is so ingrained in their mind. This is how we need to be on the subject of love. So I'm here to give you the real deal according to God.

Love looks patient and kind. Love looks honest and truthful. Love looks determined to go the distance. Love looks hopeful and enduring. Love looks like it holds on no matter what! Doesn't that sound good? Now let me tell you what love *doesn't* look like. Love doesn't look jealous or boastful or proud or rude. Love doesn't look selfish or irritable. Love doesn't get an attitude and act like the Energizer bunny, with a grudge that keeps going and going. Love doesn't look happy at other people's misfortunes. Love doesn't look like a quitter, and it never looks as if it loses faith in the object of its affections. So where did I get that list? Read 1 Corinthians 13 for yourself. It's all there. I do daresay God knows what He's talking about.

Remember, God wants women to be treated in the same way He treats us. He is the embodiment of love, and yet the Bible says, "We love Him because He first loved us." Now that's the correct order, girls! Remember when your mother told you you'd be better off with a man who loved you more than you loved him? This is where that logic comes from. Your mother's thought was that a man would always bend over backwards to please you if he loved you passionately. You, on the other hand, would never get hurt because you wouldn't be a slave to your emotions. You see, the Bible says that "God so loved the world that He *gave*." That's what love does. It is ever seeking, ever reaching out to give. If God felt giving was necessary to prove His love for us, what should we expect from men? This is not encouragement for you to use men. This is just a refresher on what true love looks like.

God's Plan for Love (The Real Deal on Love)

Let's look at what God tells husbands to do for their wives, which should let you know how serious He is about this love thing. "And you husbands must love your wives with the same love Christ showed the church. He gave up his life for her to make her holy and clean, washed by baptism and God's word.... In the same way, husbands ought to love their wives as they love their own bodies. For a man is actually loving himself when he loves his wife. No one hates his own body but lovingly cares for it, just as Christ cares for his body, which is the church.... As the Scriptures say, 'A man leaves his father and mother and is joined to his wife, and the two are united into one.' ...So again I say, each man must love his wife as he loves himself, and the wife must respect her husband" (Ephesians 5:25,26,28,29,31,33 NLT). Now is that deep or what? Let's analyze this a little further so we can be absolutely clear on the meaning of love.

God tells the man he is to love the woman sacrificially. He is to take care of her as if he is taking care of himself. Wow! This man is supposed to be responsible for her spiritually, emotionally, and physically. He is to be her priest, her provider, her lover, her friend. He is to protect her, care for her, and cover her because that is what Christ did. He is to treat her as if she is the first person in his family. Uh oh, I know I'm stepping on some toes right about now! I hear the sound of mama's boys toppling like dominoes. Yes, he has been instructed to *leave* mama and daddy and *cleave* to his wife. And needless to say, I agree with Paul's comment. It's a great mystery how two people ever get together and make love last, but when it's done God's way it truly works.

Notice that God doesn't ask the woman to love the man. He asks that she *respect* the man. And if he's doing what he's supposed to be doing, loving him won't be a problem, will it? As a matter of fact, if he's doing all the caring and nurturing he's supposed to be doing, the flame of your love will light up on automatic pilot. As for this whole submission thing, which we talk about more in a later principle, that won't be difficult either if he's doing what God ordered him to do. His actions will nurture your trust and confidence in his decision-making process. You will have the peace of mind that his judgment call for everything he does, is made with your good in mind.

Are you getting a clear picture of love yet? Let's try one more exercise. Choose someone in your life who most closely lives up to God's definition of loving you. This can be a parent, a sibling, or a friend. Make a list of the things this person does that make you feel loved. Now take that list and compare it to a list of what the man in your life does to make you feel loved. Before you get started down the wrong track, this list cannot have items on it like, "I feel tingly when he kisses me." None of that! This is not about how he makes your *flesh* feel. We're talking about love, not lust. Love reaches deeper into our souls and is more eternal than physical feelings. So save all of the mushy, touchy, feely stuff for the end of the list, and you shouldn't list more of those than his other attributes, okay?

This exercise will be futile if you aren't honest with yourself. If you have a difficult time compiling a list on him, you need to reevaluate your situation. And whatever you do, don't get all religious and spiritualize yourself out of making any earthly sense! The Lord is not going to make you marry someone you don't like in order to teach you lessons about life. Marriage is supposed to be a pleasing experience that glorifies Him, so don't go blaming God for your bad choices. I believe He told us to "try the spirits" (1 John 4:1 KJV). The bottom line is this: after you're sure this guy is a match spiritually, he should also hit three buttons in your heart before you even consider if he is husband material. You should *like* him, *love* him, and be *in love* with him. If one of those buttons doesn't work, watch and wait.

Principles women know there is no such thing as falling in love. Love is *higher* than us. It commands us to come up higher. How many of you know that the higher the staircase goes, the slower you climb in order to preserve enough energy to reach the top? When love is in sight it's worth the hike, as long as your escort looks fit and willing to go the distance and reach the goal at the top. Dare to be honest with yourself if he isn't. This is the biggest favor you can do for yourself. Please do not be like the lady who refuses to admit she needs larger shoes. She just keeps squeezing her feet into a shoe two sizes smaller, then complains that her feet hurt. Now whose fault is that? Love definitely does not look painful or uncomfortable!

Perhaps you've accepted the fact that you have big feet and you never put yourself through that type of torture. Well, what about that gorgeous suit or dress that you know doesn't fit anymore? You try sucking in your stomach and holding your breath, or rationalizing that you can wear it in the morning before you've eaten, but you just need to face it, girl. *It doesn't fit!* Let it go! Nothing looks worse on a lady than ill-fitting attire. Ever notice the funny looks and whispered comments that follow her as she goes on her way? You don't want that. Reserve that spot in your closet for something that will suit those voluptuous curves of yours. *Principles* women do not insist on hanging on to love that fits all wrong. After all, you can now see what love looks like—all the colors and shades of it. And when you drape yourself in it, you're sure to look absolutely stunning.

Prayer

Heavenly Father, thank You for the precious gift of Your love. Thank You for showing me what love looks like through the gift of Your Son. I ask that You impart to me the capacity to love as You love. Grant me the gift of discernment to see the hidden motives of the men who enter my life. Keep before me a picture of what love looks like, that I may not be deceived by the crumbs the enemy offers. Help me to wait on You to bring the one who will manifest Your love to me in human form. Until then keep my heart in the palm of Your hand for safekeeping, in Jesus' Name. Amen.

Principle #3

Get a Life!

*I*f an idle mind is the devil's workshop, then an empty life has got to be the most fabulous playground he'll ever romp across! Every type of creature loves a wide open playground. They love having the freedom to frolic about with no respect or regard for the property. And so it is on the playground of love and life. Why? Because empty spaces attract all the wrong types. Unclaimed territory is an open invitation for all kinds of undesirable individuals to squat. They have nothing to give. They're just looking for an open place to drop themselves and their garbage.

Whatever you do, do not—I repeat—*do not* sit around saying to yourself, "Well, when I get the right man my life will begin." *Not!* You better get a life! As a general rule, those who wait for others to entertain them only seem boring to those who have the ability to entertain. So make yourself interesting. That's what happens when you decide to pursue a variety of interests other than your nine-to-five job and Sunday morning church service. "But, Michelle, I've been living my life this way for a long time," you say. "I wouldn't know the first place to look to find a life if I *did* want to get one. I thought the only thing that was making my life incomplete was the absence of a man, so exactly how do I get a life?" I'm so glad you asked! The surefire way to get a life is to discover your purpose and run with it. In the book of Philippians, Paul said, "[It's] not as though I had already attained, either were already perfect: but I follow after, if that I may apprehend that for which also I am apprehended of Christ Jesus" (3:12 KJV). Another translation says, "I keep working toward that day when I will finally be all that Christ Jesus saved me for and wants me to be" (NLT).

Get Going on Your Purpose

Now we've established that you definitely were not some cosmic slip in the mind of God, that you were fearfully and wonderfully made, and that God actually made little 'ol you *on purpose*! Obviously God had very specific plans for your life. As a matter of fact, He says exactly that in Jeremiah 29:11: "'For I know the plans I have for you,' says the LORD. 'They are plans for good and not for disaster, to give you a future and a hope'" (NLT). You can bet your bottom dollar that when something is done on purpose, it stands to reason there was a need for what was done. Therefore *you* have a God-ordained purpose. "Oooh," you say with a tinge of understanding. "Where have you been?" I respond. All *Principles* women know that! That's all right, I won't hold it against you but it's time to catch up. Purposelessness may almost be as great as Jergen's lotion for the hands, but it's bad for the skin and the figure. All that inactivity can make you gain weight and break out. How many know your hands will probably be one of the last things he notices about you? All right, then. Purposelessness sets you up to think you have the sort of life you need to be rescued from. That "rescue me" mentality will cause you to leap for the wrong knight every time. You'll be happy he has a horse; you won't notice his armor is looking kinda tacky and his horse is limping. But a *Principles* woman who is leading a "purpose-full" life will have to stop and carefully consider if he is worthy of becoming a priority over some of the other details and activities in her life. This will make her far more discerning when considering the men who come her way. And you should know discernment and desperation have never been good friends. So boot out desperation, get busy with purpose, and say hello to self satisfaction.

Do you know what happens when you are satisfied and pleased with yourself? Subconsciously you begin to smile from the inside out. And while you're busy doing your thing and grinning away, some man will be attracted to the light of your smile. Remember the movie *Field of Dreams?* Kevin Costner's character kept hearing a voice telling him, "If you build it, they will come." Well, if you get a life, he will come! This is the Scripture God gave to me some time back: "After ye have done the will of God, ye might receive the promise. For yet a little while, and he that shall come will come, and will not tarry" (Hebrews 10:36 KJV). I didn't like hearing it at the time, but I do now. If you're not convinced, consider this—this is the best part of the whole equation—if it takes him a little while to arrive, you won't mind because you will be too busy to notice!

So how does a *Principles* woman find her purpose? Let me tell you a little story. Shortly after I wrote *What to Do Until Love Finds You,* my mother said to me, "I should have known you would end up doing something like this. You were always writing little poems and short stories when you were a child. I still have a notebook filled with your writings from childhood." I was amazed. I had vague memories of enjoying English class and being very excited when we were assigned creative writing homework, but I never connected writing with making a living. So as I became older and began making career choices, I didn't consider writing. I chose commercial art as a practical occupation that was enjoyable enough to hold my interest, and off I raced into the exciting world of an advertising art director. It was a beautiful thing—I didn't have to worry about spelling anything correctly again in my life!

But one day something happened. Call it fate if you will, but I like to think of it as God's invisible hand giving me a nudge back on track. At the time I was working on a tight deadline to finish an idea for a television commercial, and I couldn't find my writer. So I sat down and wrote the script myself, presented it to the board, and it sold!

Well, from that day on my boss and my supervisor conspired against me and forced me to become a writer. Notice I said *forced.* In my mind, the writing assignments they gave me were just extra work heaped on top of my art director tasks. "But I'm not a writer!" I cried. "I'm an art director; it's just not fair!" It especially didn't seem fair when I found myself writing at my desk late at night, long after I had finished my art director duties. But they turned a deaf ear to my whining and said with finality, "You are a writer and you are going to write that copy before you go home." Well, I was just too outdone...until I watched a piece of my copy come to life in a national commercial. I discovered the joy of breathing life into a thought and sharing it with others. The gift that God had deposited in me was unearthed and it began to blossom big time. Soon after I traded in my art director's table for a typewriter, and the rest is history!

If I could imagine how this whole purpose thing worked, I would picture this scenario: One day God, Jesus, and the Holy Spirit were talking and God said, "I want to minister to single people in an honest way. I want to give them heavenly advice without making it sound so lofty it will do them no earthly good. This is what I have purposed to do." At this, Jesus and the Holy Spirit got really excited because they knew this advice would be greatly needed in the future. Jesus said, "That's a fabulous concept. You need to fashion someone to wrap around that." And the Holy Spirit said, "I know that's right!" So God said, "I have the perfect person in mind. I will call her Michelle. For she will be the embodiment of her name: *Who is like God? One who stands behind and practices absolute truth.* In other words, she'll be crazy enough to tell it like it is." On that note I entered the picture and, despite getting distracted away from God's agenda by my own personal agenda, I eventually began the work that God had created me to do. Thank God that nothing can deter our determined Father from accomplishing what He ordains!

Follow Your Heart

So many times we lay aside our original dreams in pursuit of a safer path. "I've got to make a living; that will just have to be a hobby," we say. This statement makes our life comfortable but boring. I firmly believe that when we dare to reach past what is practical and follow the beat of our heart, we are sure to arrive at the place of success and prosperity. The other symptom of not living out our purpose is the feeling that we're never appreciated. It's like wearing a stunning evening dress to work. It may look marvelous, but it's glaringly out of place. That overshadows the beauty of the dress and, sadly, the outfit does not obtain the appreciation it deserves. Like the dress, we don't get our full share of appreciation when we function outside of our real purpose.

What did you dream of doing when you were a child? What makes your heart truly happy? Are you doing it? Why not? If finances are a problem, can you begin doing something bit by bit to reach your goal? Believe me, when God sees that you are serious He will make a way to get you back on track. After all, that dream in your heart was His idea first! Remember, when God gives a commission He also makes a provision. But He needs you to take that first step.

Once you step smack-dab into the middle of your purpose, an extraordinary thing will happen. You'll hear a heavenly drum roll and a voice will thunder, "Congratulations! You now have a life!" Then everyone around you will applaud and you'll begin to feel very pleased with yourself. Just be careful you don't get full of yourself. However, it *is* proper for a *Principles* woman to let her soul be filled with the promises and fulfillment of God's plans for her life. After all, "A satisfied soul loathes the honeycomb, but to a hungry soul every bitter thing is sweet" (Proverbs 27:7 NKJV). That means you can take it or leave it, you don't have to have it *because you are already satisfied.*

We can look at the book of Ruth to see a *Principles* woman at work. Remember how Boaz was checking Ruth out from afar and she didn't have a clue? She was too busy gathering food. Naomi had to sit her down and say, "You better take another look at this man." You know the rest of the story, and if you don't, you should definitely read it. Ruth didn't sit around whining about the lack of a man in her life; she got on with her life and love intercepted her. Her hands were completely open, and that put her in the position to receive. Perhaps this is why Jesus said, "If you cling to your life, you will lose it; but if you give it up for me, you will find it" (Matthew 10:39 NLT).

Get Busy!

So what's the bottom line? *Principles* women who get busy about the business of their God-ordained purpose are happy people.

And happy people attract other happy people—people who are genuinely interested in bringing something good to the party.

Go ahead, pursue that dream you buried. Take that trip you always wanted to take. Buy that bauble. Take that class. Go to that museum. Collect experiences that will make you fascinating. Grab hold of life, throw it around your shoulders, and strut your stuff. *Principles* women know that a full life is a thing of rare beauty, so treasure every moment of it.

Prayer

Heavenly Father, this day I resubmit my life to You. I ask that You dismantle every previous dream and goal that I have clung to that is not of You, and replace them with Your vision for my life. I ask that You reveal Your ordained purpose for my life and give me the courage to follow it through. I ask that You would plant Your desire for my life so firmly in my spirit that it burns like a fire that consumes me with a zeal to do Your bidding. Make provision for Your commission for my life. Fill my life with Yourself, fill every empty space in me with a sense of divine purpose and love for You. Let me be found being busy about my Father's business with joy emanating from my soul as I bask in the knowledge that I am in the center of Your will, in Jesus Name. Amen.

Principle #4

Mind Your Own Business

*H*ave you ever walked from one room to another in order to get something, then completely forgotten what it was you went to get? What did you do next? I'll tell you what you did. You walked *allll* the way back into the other room and as soon as you sat down you remembered what it was you went to get. So you went *allll* the way back to the other room to get it! Something happens when we get too focused on what we're trying to find—we completely lose it. Only when we relax do things begin to happen. Now tell me the truth, if you really were "waiting to exhale," would you still be alive?

Let Him Find You First

The world has convinced us women that we are not fully functioning, fulfilled individuals without a man. What can you say when popular artists make desperation . sound so good? Songs declare "there's no me without you" or "if love ends then I promise you that I shall never breathe again." *Puh-leeze!* That's what I say. C'mon, if our ability to breathe depended on a man being in our lives, the world would have an epidemic of dead women, and I would be among them. How about you?

Actually, it's the other way around. The wrong relationship can squeeze the very life out of you. That's why it's so important to allow God to choose the man that He wants to find you. Notice I said that He finds you. Yes, indeed! My Bible tells me, "When a man finds a wife, he finds a good thing" (see Proverbs 18:22). This always was, and always will be, the perfect order of a relationship because it is spiritual law. So don't get indignant and tell me, hey, Michelle, this is the nineties. God couldn't care less what year it is. He and His word remain constant, and that's for a very good reason.

So where did God come up with the idea that the man finds the woman? Believe it or not, He arranged this in order to give the woman power. Let's face it—men never appreciate anything they don't have to work for to get. The spirit of conquest is in the heart of every man. Small wonder if they're not on the field, they're in front of the television, totally hypnotized by the sight of other men jumping all over each other for a little ball. Grown men have cried shamelessly for the world to see after winning a championship. They've kissed the trophy, kissed each other…oh, brother! Get the picture? Men reverence that which is hard-earned. God wanted women to be appreciated in the same way. This would ensure that we receive the special treatment He knew we deserved. The only way to make certain this happened was to establish specific rules in the game of love. So relax—take a seat behind the end zone and let him come and get you.

That's all your mother was trying to tell you when she told you not to call boys. When you were young and got into the habit of calling boys, their response was often crude because they were too young to know what to say. They got bored after a while and usually didn't bother to tell you they'd had enough; they just began acting strange, eventually moved on, and avoided you until you got the painful message. Now that you're older, men have more polish but sometimes they still avoid being honest. They will actually cooperate with you for a time as long as it's convenient for them. But eventually they meet a greater challenge that intrigues them, and they come up with some smooth way to slither out of the picture. I'm sure this is where the expression "Men are snakes" came from. But this could never happen if we women hadn't paved the way.

When women go in pursuit of men they end up like the Shulamite woman—on the wrong side of town, in the dark, badly wounded, with a torn veil. But when she decided to "tend to," as the old folks say—as in *tend to her own garden*—she found herself surrounded by the chariots of her lover. Read Song of Songs. That's the way you want a man to talk about you. Talk about art appreciation! My goodness!

But let me break this down a little. The wrong side of town is out of your jurisdiction, out of your God-designed role. Being in the dark means being confused. You won't have a clue as to who really wants who if you did all the work to make it happen! Besides, this just leads to insecurity, and insecurity makes you do foolish things that will eventually drive him away. Being badly wounded is the end result of it all. And a torn veil is indicative of being exposed to disgrace, which leaves you open to a spirit of bitterness and rejection.

Okay, now for all of my nineties women who want to puff up their chests and tell me how liberated they are and that "this is no longer a man's world; we've come a long way baby; this is the year of the woman..." There is nothing new about that conversation. It's *always* been the year of the woman because men would be nothing without us! God Himself declared that man needed help, and we were made for that purpose—to be a sort of business partner, not a doormat, so get your theology straight and calm down.

"Well, I don't want to play games!" you say. Who said anything about playing games? If you've been taking art appreciation and getting a life, you won't have time to run after some man. He'll have to make an effort to seek you out because you—a *Principles* woman—will be too busy minding your own business! You see, men are not ultimately inclined to make a commitment. They generally only commit in order to acquire. Therefore, your life should be full of activity and interests apart from him. He should be compelled to decide that the only way he will be able to capture your attention and time consistently is to marry you. The more available you make yourself, the further away your wedding day will be—end of story.

Rebecca is another wonderful example of a *Principles* woman in action. She was busy drawing water for her father's household when Abraham's servant spotted her and decided she would be a perfect match for Isaac. Here Rebecca was doing her usual tasks on a seemingly ordinary day and then *bam!* All of a sudden she was showered with expensive gifts and carried away to meet her rich husband. Sounds like a happy ending to me. Read Genesis chapter 24 for yourself. Notice what Rebecca was doing—seeing to the refreshment of her father's household. Who is our father? Abba, Father God! As we, too, yield to being about our Father's business and seeking first the kingdom of God and His righteousness, He will make sure that all good things will be added unto us (Matthew 6:33). I know a lot of singles are sick of this Scripture but it's the truth. Sorry, there's no way around this precept. Nothing that will amount to anything joyful, that is.

Do Things by God's Design

It's time to admit that our little hard-headed ways are not working. Marching to the world's beat and philosophies will only lead us farther and farther away from our God-given heart's desire. *Principles* women know it profits them to do things by God's design. And God never intended for the woman to make the relationship happen. The original design was for the man to pour out and the woman to receive and produce the fruit of that man's labor of love. And so the circle of love would ever expand with everyone joyfully fulfilling their part.

So stop fighting the notion that men and women are different! It takes one look at yourself in the buff to settle that argument. This is not a negative thing. Our differences—physical, mental, and spiritual—are to be celebrated. We were fashioned on purpose to balance one another perfectly. So the conclusion is simple: Man needs woman and woman needs man in order for both to be complete. But a man will only recognize his need for you if he notices that there is a gaping hole in his life caused by your absence. Give him a chance to miss you. Give him a chance to long for you. You have nothing to lose and everything to gain.

Sometimes it takes men a little while to figure out exactly what they need, so they go off to name all the animals first, like Adam did. But by the time he finished that exercise he had no problem recognizing Eve as his missing rib. Her initial absence made the difference startlingly clear. By the time he discovered her, he knew that she was definitely the one. That's the position you want to be in. If self-control becomes too difficult for you to maintain, meditate on this Scripture: "Who can find a virtuous woman? for her price is far above rubies" (Proverbs 31:10 KJV).

Have you ever been jewelry shopping and had some marvelous little trinket catch your eye? You tried it on and couldn't bear to leave it behind. You had to have it, and you were willing to bust your budget for it. Meanwhile that little gem didn't beg you to take it home. It just sat on your finger being what it is, simply, resplendently beautiful. If you are a *Principles* woman, you are that gem! So remember that, to some extent, this search for the perfect mate is like a treasure hunt. It's important to be clear about your role. You are the treasure; he is the hunter. So just sit still and sparkle, girl!

Prayer

Heavenly Father, help me to trust that You are able to deliver all that my heart longs for. Let my expectation be from You and not what my own efforts can grasp. Give me a heart of confidence in my own desirability and value. Help me to stay in position, constantly before You, as You bring the mate that You have chosen for me into my life. Help me to walk in the spirit, releasing myself to him only at Your instruction. Let Your will for my life be realized, in Jesus' Name. Amen.

Principle #5

Develop Good Shopping Skills

Now that we've established that it's the man who does the finding and pursuing, let us also lay the groundwork for what should take place after he's approached you. This is when the dating process begins. Let's be perfectly clear from the top. Dating does *not* mean mating. There is no purchase required in dating. Dating is a specific season in the relationship designated for gathering information or data, not goose bumps. Why information? Because, should the relationship go further into the realm of marriage, this is the foundation you'll be building on for the rest of your life. You need information. You need specs. You need to know how much this relationship is going to cost and what the profit margin will be before you can decide if it will be a good investment. After all, "which of you, intending to build a tower, sitteth not down first, and counteth the cost, whether he have sufficient to finish it?" (Luke 14:28 KJV).

This is why I like to compare shopping to dating. Both can get you in trouble if you don't know what you want before you leave home. You'll either end up coming home empty-handed or carrying a bunch of stuff you don't need. Not finding anything leaves you feeling frustrated, and buying what you don't need leaves you feeling guilty, especially if it's a non-refundable purchase! You can go for broke with both shopping and dating. One will affect your wallet, the other will affect something more important—your heart.

So you say you're in the market for a husband? Let me give you some simple guidelines that should not be ignored. After all, this is one outfit you can't just take back to the store. This purchase will affect the rest of your life. Therefore, you need to stick to your shopping list and not get tempted by men simply because they look like a bargain. Forget about it! *Principles* women don't have that kind of time or emotional energy to waste. They know it's important to "Keep your heart with all diligence, for out of it spring the issues of life" (Proverbs 4:23 NKJV).

Check the Label

On that note, first things first. Check the designer label. Is he a self-made man or a vessel fashioned and yielded to the Lord? You do not want a spiritual knockoff, okay? If this man isn't completely sold out to God, leave him in the dressing room! Let the salesgirl put him away. Write this on a tablet in your heart: if a man is not submitted to God, he will not have the capacity to love you the way you want to be loved. He will be moving in his own understanding instead of being led by the Spirit of God. This leaves you at the mercy of someone who has no accountability to anyone, other than himself, for his actions. This is *not* what you want. You want a man whose heart is so tender and tuned in to God that when he does decide to clown, God will tap him on the shoulder and say, "Hey, buddy, you know that wasn't right. Go back to her and apologize. Fix it before I fix you." And he knows what that means, so he makes his way back to you and repents. That's the kind of man you want!

Feel the Fabric

Next check out the fabric of the man. What's he made of? Does he possess character, integrity, wisdom, and compassion?

How is his relationship with his family? How about his friends? Come on, now, this is the person who will be leading your household! You want someone you will respect enough to trust in that position. How does he hold up in the middle of a trial? Is he one-hundred percent pure blessing? You know, some synthetic blends you can buy these days look beautiful the first few times you wear them, but after a few washings and pressings they begin to ball up and look worse for the wear. That's when a marriage begins to look tacky, and you begin to appear a bit worn around the edges. So make sure that man is cut from the right cloth!

Get a Good Fit

Obviously, the fit is very important. Nothing looks worse than ill-fitting clothing, with the exception of an ill-fitting relationship. Since you've completed your course on Art Appreciation and gotten a life, you should be able to figure out if this man fits into God's design for your future. Are your goals complementary? You need to find out if both of you are going in the same direction. "Can two walk together, except they be agreed?" (Amos 3:3 KJV).

Remember when hitchhiking was popular? A motorist would stop and ask the person on the side of the road which direction he wanted to go. If the hitchhiker was going their way, the driver would give him a ride. If not, the driver would say, "Sorry, I'm not going in that direction." The car would then move on, leaving the hitchhiker on the side of the road to wait for someone who was going his way. Get the concept? Do not be fooled! After the romance wears off you'll want to jump back into the business of living out your dreams, and if you find yourself with someone who is not in agreement with you, this will be the beginning of great difficulty for you both. You will consider him a hindrance rather than a help. Now, that's not an ideal wardrobe choice, is it?

Make sure this man fits your lifestyle and goes with the rest of the wardrobe you already have hanging in the closet of your life. And remember, unlike a skirt, there is no such thing as altering a human being. Only the Holy Spirit can do that. So understand going in that this is an "as is" purchase. Can you live with the flaws? Speak now or forever hold your peace because this is a final sale!

Take a Look at Your Budget

Can we discuss everyone's favorite subject? You got it, finances. Check your budget. Is this relationship too costly spiritually, emotionally, or physically? Or is it making you a richer person? This one calls for hard-core honesty. Do you "consider how to stimulate one another to love and good deeds?" (Hebrews 10:24 NASB). God's design is that your relationship should make you more effective in service to Him. Your union is all about displaying kingdom living and glorifying Him in the world by your example. And you thought marriage was just about you falling in love and having a good time, didn't you?

Well, my friend, look at it this way. When you buy an outfit and put it on, you're not the only person who sees it. Everyone around you sees it. And, depending on what they see, they will all have an opinion of that outfit that they might—or might not—share with you. However, they most likely will share that opinion with someone else. I'm sure none of us goes shopping with the goal of buying something so atrocious that we turn off the masses when we go out into the world wearing it. Naturally, you'd like to look your best. For the sake of the kingdom, and our heavenly Father's sake, *Principles* women cannot afford to make the costly mistake of a blind purchase. We must examine the merchandise closely and make wise investments with our hearts.

Don't Shop When You're Hungry

Last, but certainly not least, never, ever go shopping when you're hungry! You're bound to scoop up something you don't need. Then later, when you come to your senses, you'll be standing there scratching your head and wondering, "Why? How? And why didn't anybody tell me?" And the truth of the matter is, someone probably *did* try to tell you, but you were too far gone because the voice of your needs drowned out the sound of good advice. So recognize when you're feeling desperate and give up shopping until the hunger pains fade away. The Lord encourages us to hearken diligently unto Him and "eat ye that which is good, and let your soul delight itself in fatness" (Isaiah 55:2 KJV). When your soul is full, even the juiciest-looking male won't tempt you to impulse shop. You'll be able to check him out in an objective manner.

Talk to Your Personal Shopper

And when in doubt about a purchase, the best fashion consultant and interior decorator (for your heart, you see) I know of is the Holy Spirit. He promises that "whether you turn to the left or the right, your ears will hear a voice behind you saying, 'This is the way, walk ye in it'" (Isaiah 30:21 KJV). Wow! You have your very own personal shopper! And believe me, He knows exactly what you need, so definitely check with Him before making any purchases. It may be true that it's the man who finds the woman, but every man who comes your way will not be your husband. *Principles* women know how to balance heavenly discernment with good, practical, down-to-earth sense. Therefore, the choice is still up to us as to whether or not he gets to take us home!

Prayer

Heavenly Father, Your Word says that if we lack wisdom we should ask You. Therefore, I come into Your presence with thanksgiving and rejoice in all You offer me as Your child. I ask that You grant me the gifts of keen insight and perception. Let Your wisdom rule the decisions of my heart. Keep my ears open to the leading of Your Spirit. Open my eyes to see men as they really are, and make wise decisions accordingly. Help me to be willing to stand alone, trusting You to deliver what's best for me. Give me the strength to walk according to Your revelation and not by my own understanding or desires. Help me to rest in Your love as I wait for your God-sent choice for me, in Jesus' Name. Amen.

Principle #6

Avoid the Mission Field

So you want to win souls for the Kingdom? That is a wonderful desire which is pleasing to God...*unless!* Unless your missionary endeavors are solely focused on some unsaved man who you are interested in. If you're driving down that highway, put on the brakes now! You are headed for a crash. Been there, done that! I could tell you all about it, but it's too horrifying. Well, okay, just one story...Mmmm, how about a general overview? To get any more specific would be downright embarassing. You might say at one point in my life I was the diva of missionary dating. In the face of my friend's upraised eyebrows and disapproving clucks I announced I could handle it and marched off into the arms of all the wrong kinds of men. Sure they were cute enough, exciting enough, and certainly romantic enough, but at the end of the day there was always some dramatic explosion that ruined the fun. Years ago a singer by the name of Vanity sang the words, "He made such a pretty mess of my dress" (or something like that). But the bottom line is, a mess is never pretty. Courting the world can make a mess of your salvation and your witness, and leave you looking worse for wear. After several experiences that all started well enough but ended painfully, I decided the mission field was not for me.

I know all the rationalizations: *Then why did God allow this person to come into my life if he didn't want me to minister to him? Well, there aren't any saved men around. The men in the world seem to be much more interesting and attractive than the men in the church.* Should I keep going? Let me share with you the answers to those excuses for dating an unbeliever. Don't try to blame your disobedience on God. Life happens! We are not exempt from unfruitful encounters. That's why the Lord gave us guidelines to follow, and you're a big girl now. Deal with the situation by referring that cute guy to a brother in Christ who can minister to him effectively. You'll find out real fast how interested he is in the things of God!

Secondly, you're beginning to sound like Elisha's servant. Remember when he panicked and thought his people were outnumbered by the enemy? Elisha was quick to reassure him that "they that be with us are more than they that be with them" (2 Kings 6:16 KJV). It's true! God has a myriad of saved men. But you only need *one*, and he will be released to find you, or recognize you, in the fullness of God's time.

Lastly, of course those men in the world are cute if you're only looking on the outside! If that's the case, Satan is cute too. The Bible says he comes disguised as an angel of light (2 Corinthians 11:14). The devil is an expert at making himself and his servants look attractive. After all, beauty is a surface thing. You've seen enough before-and-after makeup demonstration photos to know that. So whenever your eyeballs start to wander and linger on some cutie who is not of the spiritual persuasion (meaning blood-bought and sold out to God, not following some esoteric system of beliefs), you need to snap to, pinch yourself, and do whatever it takes to remember that "Charm is deceitful and beauty is vain, but a woman who fears the LORD, she shall be praised" (Proverbs 31:30 NASB). And keep in mind that goes for men, too!

Don't Hook Up with an Unsaved Man

So why did God say, "Be ye not unequally yoked together with unbelievers: for what fellowship hath righteousness with unrighteousness? and what communion hath light with darkness?" (2 Corinthians 6:14 KJV). I know the answer to that: none at all. How can you get so impatient and frustrated with your family members who refuse to get saved, then run straight into the arms of an unsaved man? Is there really any difference? Like your unsaved family members, he doesn't get what you're talking about when you start sharing the things of God. He's just going along with the program to get what he wants. Oh yes, men in the world know that women in the church are a good catch! After all is said and done, they're looking for well-kept women too. They know they don't have to worry about your morals because you answer to God. Well, that's good for him, but what about you? Who is he accountable to besides his own flesh? What is your assurance that he can be trusted with your heart? Think about it!

Samson learned this lesson the hard way. He lo-o-oved unsaved women. And they brought him a lot of trouble! Most people only think of the Delilah story when Samson's name comes up. But Delilah was the last in a line of Philistine women who had very similar traits. These women had no regard for Samson's God-ordained purpose. They couldn't be trusted. They sold him out to the enemy and ultimately caused his death.

Don't fool yourself. You will have a hard time living a godly life with an unsaved man. You're only human. Because it is impossible for the weaker one to keep up, it's a natural instinct for one who is stronger to step back in order to fall in step with the one who is weaker. You'll be the only one making adjustments in your walk, which will be a bad witness, which will make him lose respect for you, which will make you feel bad, which will affect the relationship, which will eventually unravel beyond repair.... Do you see where this is going?

Major in the Beauty of Holiness

Perhaps you need to take a second course in Art Appreciation—one that majors in the beauty of holiness. I've heard it said that most women marry carbon copies of their fathers. This could be a good thing or a bad thing, depending on the father. *Principles* women should definitely keep their eye open for a man who looks like Daddy. Like our Abba Father. Our heavenly Father. A man who is righteous and who walks in the power of the Spirit. Now that's a fine specimen of a man who will make your life exciting! And it won't matter what he looks like; he'll be cute to you because you will be *in love.* And love covers a multitude of imperfections, as well as sins.

My happiest married friends all say that the man they married was not their type physically. Sometimes he just wasn't their type, period. But honey, you can't peel them away from that man now! And don't try to tell them their husband isn't cute. In their eyes, he's the finest thing walking! Why the sudden transformation? Because these women married godly men—men surrendered to God's precepts on caring for a woman. And who could ever resist a helping of love topped with the best treatment?

Also, there's something pretty irresistible about a man who can pray. Whose heart is tender. Who walks in spiritual sensitivity. You know you're covered. He's got your back. He can call down God and chase away the devil. He can cover you and love you like no other because he is manifesting the love of God that the world will never comprehend. You'll share a level of intimacy with this man that has to be experienced to be believed. A man in the world won't be able to scratch the surface of this kind of deep love!

So don't miss a blessing by looking for the wrong thing: "For man looks on the outward appearance, but the LORD looks at the heart" (1 Samuel 16:7 NASB). Samuel would have missed a fantastic king if he hadn't listened to God. At first he went looking for some tall, striking figure of a man to crown as King of Israel. But it was David—a lowly shepherd boy, the youngest and seemingly most insignificant of them all—who rose to power as the most spectacular king in the history of Israel.

Mothers used to instruct their daughters, "This one has potential. If you work with this one, you'll have a winner on your hands." Well, that certainly doesn't happen anymore! Women today want their men to arrive camera-ready! But who said you were perfect? Don't think about changing or rearranging him. Concentrate on inspiring him and empowering him to rise up and be all that God has ordained him to be. Some women I know have initially passed right by their husbands because he wasn't perfectly polished. You don't think all these successful men in the world started off that way, do you? Of course not! They climbed and climbed until they reached their goal. And most likely some woman was right there beside him all the way. Now those women get to reap the rewards. And that reward is so much greater if he's a man of God.

So if your missionary vision spans from America's inner cities to Papua, New Guinea, by all means follow your heart! But missionary dating should definitely be a field that is off-limits. You'll find too many weeds growing there that will trip and choke you. Stick to the straight and narrow path, and you'll see him coming in the distance. Before you know it he will be right next to you. And you'll recognize him because he'll look just like your Daddy.

Prayer

Dear Heavenly Father, give me a heart that wants what You want for me. I ask that You help me not to judge by outward appearances, but by the heart. Open my eyes to see beauty and value where You see them. Give me a heart that won't settle for less than Your chosen vessel of love for me, in Jesus' Name. Amen.

Principle #7

Protect Your Jewels

$\mathcal{A}$nyone who has been the victim of a rob-
bery has described the experience as trau-
matic and violating. Whether it is your body, your home, or your
heart that's been robbed, the pain and horror of it lingers long after
the initial shock. You're not able to trust strangers and you find
yourself frightened and nervous for quite some time.

I experienced these feelings firsthand not too long ago. I was
walking across the street one day when a man, who was stopped at
a stop sign, stepped on his gas pedal as I walked in front of his car.
And it didn't end there. He kept going! Because of the force of the
vehicle I was not able to get out of the way, and I was literally
straddling the front of his van, screaming for him to stop.
Eventually I couldn't hold on any longer so I fell and rolled into
the street, only to look up and see his van still coming toward me.
With no hope of rolling out of the way in time, I screamed "Jesus!"
and he screeched to a stop right in front of my feet.

He missed running over me completely by mere inches. My leg was severely injured. After three operations, and a year and a half of being pretty much bed-bound except for my visits to my physical therapist, I found myself terrified to cross the street. I no longer trusted that people would come to a halt at stop signs. At crosswalks, the light would change, people would walk across, and I—paralyzed by fear—would still be standing there. Fortunately, I had very understanding friends to help me through this difficult time. I had been violated and injured by the carelessness of someone else. And I was afraid, unwilling to take any chances that would make me a victim again.

This is what happens when men hurt us. After several bad experiences most of us shut down entirely. About that time some really nice man comes ambling around the corner and reaches out to us, and we shrink back as if someone poured acid on us! We're unable to respond, we have nothing left to give. We've been robbed of our self-esteem because our hearts have been violated and shattered too many times before. We're no longer willing to share any of the crumbs of our heart that might be left. That poor man moves on, scratching his head and wondering what happened. And our reaction might cause him to hurt the next woman he meets, continuing the vicious cycle. It's a fact that hurt people hurt other people.

Don't Give Too Much, Too Soon

"I gave myself to him, and he threw my love back in my face as if it were a piece of trash." How many times have you heard that comment or sounded it yourself? The truth is, most women give too much, too soon. They immediately tell men too much about their past experiences and overload them with too much present emotional data. Remember when your mother told you it behooves you to be a tad mysterious with men? She was right! A man wants you to be honest, but he doesn't want you to be *that* honest. Do you really want to hear about all *his* past relationships? *All* of them? Sometimes that information can be helpful, but sometimes it can be damaging. Anyway, it's safer for you to have more data on him than he has on you. Let me first explain that this is not about being deceitful. It's about judging what information his heart can handle without him looking at you in a judgmental light.

It seems to be more acceptable for a man to speak about all of his past relationships because society (the world at large) generally promotes this type of behavior on a man's part. However, deep within a man's psyche *he's* still in search of a virgin to marry. He might play around with a loose woman, but when it comes to marrying her he wants a woman he can trust. He is in search of a *Principles* woman. When you tell him about all your past relationships, he stores that information and it colors his view of you. After all, you are a *Principles* woman, you're not supposed to do that. You were supposed to be sitting somewhere, praying and waiting for him. And while God is faithful to forgive your past mistakes in relationships, men have a harder time with that. So while he's sitting there spilling his guts to you about all his past problems with women, don't take that as a cue to spill all your beans. Keep your business to yourself, that's why it's called *your business!* Just nod understandingly, learn what you can about him from what he tells you, and say, "Well, we all have had bad experiences, and hopefully we learned from them." *Next!*

Remember that part in Song of Songs right before the Shulamite woman was about to marry the king? Her brothers came to her and questioned her on the state of her purity. They asked if she had been a door opening to other men, or if she had been a wall keeping herself for her husband. Her brothers said that if she had been a door they would surround her with cedar, a material used for burial. But if she had been a wall they would build silver—honor—upon her. She was able to tell them that she indeed had been a wall. And her husband-to-be was proud to proclaim, "You are like a private garden, my treasure, my bride! You are like a spring that no one else can drink from, a fountain of my own" (Song of Songs 4:12 NLT). This is what *every* man would like to think of the woman he has chosen to be his wife.

When to Share Yourself
(or A Time and a Place to Share)

There is a time and a place for sharing things that will directly affect your relationship down the road should you get married. Well into your relationship you'll certainly want to share things such as physical problems, debts, and concerns. But don't share these things in the early stages of forming a friendship, especially if there's a chance of nothing happening between the two of you. You'll just be handing him too much intimate information about yourself, that he might not feel obligated to keep to himself if he's made no emotional investment in you!

Whatever you do, do not sit him down and unravel every horror story of rejection you've ever experienced. This will only make him feel that he may have made a mistake when he became interested in you. If nobody else wanted you, why should he? Don't pave a playground for the devil to do cartwheels across. You can very generally admit that you've been hurt before but God has been gracious and healing. This moves him into the area of wanting to protect your heart. Men like to feel needed. They just don't want to be drained to the dregs by your needs. Don't give him too much responsibility for your heart too soon. If he hasn't decided to commit to you, it will be too much weight for him to carry.

I know that the temptation to give a man a preview of life with you is great, but it's a very bad idea. Remember when your mom said, "Why buy the cow if you can get the milk for free?" Mmm hmm, I thought you knew! Don't behave like you're his wife if you're only his girlfriend, and don't behave like his girlfriend if you're only his friend. Got it? It's never smart to move ahead of the man's—or God's—agenda. Moving ahead only leaves you open to experience the pain of rejection. If you were going to the Caribbean in the middle of winter, you wouldn't start stripping off your sweaters and coats and putting on your bikini until you got there! Common sense tells you that walking around in a bikini in ten-degree weather will make you a very sick puppy.

On the other hand, don't be his mother or his nurse if you want to be his woman. Be kind, be nice, be supportive, but leave some room for him to keep coming toward you. Men are naturally independent beings. Remember who first noticed that Adam was alone? God did, not Adam! Adam didn't even notice, and when he finally realized what God had in mind for him he went looking in all the wrong places. So God had to knock him out in order to give him the person he had in mind for him. I tell you, the gene pool is a deep thing, because today's man is still behaving like Adam. Which means that you—a *Principles* woman—can't make life so comfortable for him that he doesn't understand that he needs to commit to marriage in order to enjoy the full benefits of life with you.

Let Him Take the Lead

This is another reason why it's smart to keep your feelings and emotions to yourself until you have a clear read on his love for you. Why is this crucial? Because whenever a woman takes the lead in a relationship, whether it is doing the calling, suggesting a date, or professing love, the devil takes your good intentions and turns them into wrong impressions. Suddenly, an impulsive move of good will on your part is interpreted as you closing in on him or chasing him. All those cute cards, surprises, thoughtful gifts, etc., become a vise that threatens to squeeze the life out of the interest he has in you. He becomes overwhelmed with the responsibility of deciding quickly to commit, even though he is not yet ready. This triggers panic in his heart, and he begins to fight for space in order to grab some control of the relationship. He needs to sort through his feelings for you *without* your help. That way, the only voices he'll hear will be his own and the Holy Spirit's.

I remember making this mistake with a man who truly loved me but realized it too late. I had no one but myself to blame because I kept telling him, "Why are you fighting this thing I know you love me—it shows in everything you do. Everybody knows it but you." So in rebellion he stomped off into another relationship to prove me wrong. I was hurt; he was miserable but too proud to untangle himself from the mess he landed in. After three years of sheer torture, he extricated himself from a bad marriage and positioned himself at my door. But too many tears and too much water had passed under the bridge to retreive what we once had.

As the Bible says, "Don't demand an audience with the king or push for a place among the great. It is better to wait for an invitation than to be sent to the end of the line, publicly disgraced" (Proverbs 25:6-7 NLT).

I think this holds true in relationships as well. When we try to hurry the process and get that man to feel what we're feeling, when we invite ourselves into a position in his life that he hasn't invited us to be in, we're headed for rejection. Think of how you feel when you're pressured by a salesperson. You're turned off whether you're interested in the product or not. You certainly do not want to be seen in that light! You're a "good thing," remember? So relax and let him take the lead.

Be Careful Where You Place Your Heart

Lastly, don't remain in situations where it's clear that you're not being appreciated for the gift that you are. A man I was dating some time back told me, "I bless the day you were born, I bless the womb that carried you." That's deep, isn't it? That should be the way your man looks at you, not as if he's doing you a favor by hanging around and gracing you with the privilege of loving him. Get rid of that man! The Bible tells us not to "cast [our] pearls before swine, lest they trample them under their feet, and turn again and rend you" (Matthew 7:6 KJV).

How many of you have had your heart walked all over, and then—just when you thought it was over—you watched that man turn around, pick your heart up off the floor while it still had his footprints all over it, tear it to shreds, and throw it in your face? This is only done by a man who never understood your value. He wouldn't recognize love if it walked up to him, slapped him on the head, and spelled out its name. Who needs this guy? You haven't been waiting this long to settle for that type of bad treatment. The earlier you see this man as he is and cut him loose, the more of your heart you'll be able to salvage.

Our poor little hearts go through so much! And it happens because we refuse to take better care of them. Proverbs 4:23 tells us to "Keep your heart[s] with all diligence, for out of it spring the issues of life" (NKJV). Yet we throw our hearts around expecting men to catch them with all abandon. And then when they fall splat on the floor of our expectations, we stand looking mortified, not comprehending what happened.

Principles women have grown to understand that there is only One who can be trusted to hold our hearts. He treats us with the tenderness we deserve. "He is able to keep that which I have committed unto him against that day" (2 Timothy 1:12 KJV). Against that day when He grants us permission to release it, and share it with the person He has ordained for our lives. Until then I suggest that you treat your heart like you would a priceless jewel. Put it away in a safe place, far from the lustful eyes of mere robbers. Lock it up and give the key to God!

Prayer

Dear Lord, as I commit my heart into Your care, keep it safe within Your hands according to Your Word. Teach me how to draw near to You. As I give my hurts and expectations to You, heal me and grant me the desires of my heart as You have promised. I place all that I am, and all that I long for, at Your feet. Be my comfort, my guide, and my confidante. Show me the beauty of drawing near to You and the peace and fulfillment that can be found in making You the center of my joy, in Jesus' Name. Amen.

Principle #8

Use a Lot of Seasoning

*A*ll right," you say, "you've told me everything not to say, so what's left to say to this man?" A lot! But it probably calls for some rearranging of your thought life. Take time to think of things which are true, honest, just, pure, lovely, of a good report, if there be any virtue or praise in the person that you are dealing with, think on these things. (That's a paraphrase of Philippians 4:8.) For most of us who have had unsatisfactory relationships or painful encounters, the residue from past conflicts has a tendency to seep out into our conversations with the nice man we just met. Our suspicions from former disappointments thwart our ability to be the blessing we could be. If only women could fully realize how much power they really have in the lives of men!

You've Got the Power

I've said it before and I'll say it again. Women have the power to make or break a man, power to build them up or tear them down—I mean, *completely* level their confidence down below sea level! For all you women out there who are interested in some guy who is basically a good man, whose only problem seems to be that he doesn't have any money, let me tell you a secret. Your words can make the man in your life wealthy. If you encourage him and have confidence in his abilities, boyfriend will start beating his chest like Tarzan and go forth and conquer his world. He'll be like the little engine who kept saying, "I think I can, I think I can, I think I can," just because you told him he could! Water may seek its own level, but men will rise to the occasion when they are encouraged.

Proverbs 31 says that the husband of the virtuous woman was known in the gates because of her. What does that say about her? That says that she pumped her husband up and made him look good. That her house was in order as a witness to his friends, and in return for her hard work and diligence he rose up and praised her. He knew how blessed he was and he told her so. Men are drawn to positive women. Anytime my friends—male and female—are feeling down, I hear from them because I'm told that I'm an encourager.

Several men who have been in my life will tell you I made them wealthy by exhorting them to use their gifts and launch out into the deep. Wherever I could network and put in a good word on their behalf, I have done so. Sparingly, mind you, because men still like to feel that they accomplished their goal by their own efforts. Men don't mind you nudging gently, but they resent you pushing or controlling their movements. That's when you lose your sex appeal and start to resemble their mother. And men aren't interested in marrying their mother, okay?

Whenever women begin complaining about how worthless men are, I feel like screaming, "Stop it! You are creating your world with the things that are coming out of your mouth." Remember this one? It was a big catch phrase during the eighties, but it seems to have been pushed to the back of the cupboard. "Death and life are in the power of the tongue" (Proverbs 18:21 NKJV). How about this one? "Likewise the tongue is a small part of the body, but it makes great boasts. Consider what a great forest is set on fire by a small spark. The tongue also is a fire…. It corrupts the whole person, sets the whole course of his life on fire…. With the tongue we praise our Lord and Father, and with it we curse men, who have been made in God's likeness. Out of the same mouth come praise and cursing. My brothers, this should not be" (James 3:5-6,9-10 NIV). *My sisters, this should not be!* Just because no one's been preaching it lately, doesn't mean that God has erased it from His word. It's still there. The law of the tongue is still in effect.

The Best Kind of Seasoning

Think about how you feel when you hang around people who are always negative. That's how the man in your life feels when you are constantly raining on his parade or bemoaning your own lot in life. Cut it out, and get positive! "Let your conversation be always full of grace, seasoned with salt, so that you may know how to answer everyone" (Colossians 4:6 NIV).

Let's talk about salt. Salt does several things. First of all, it makes you thirsty. Likewise, your conversation should make the man in your life thirsty for more of you. If you're talking the right talk, his heart will be longing after you because he feels happy when he's in your presence.

Secondly, salt makes things taste good. Your conversation should be the ingredient that makes a bland, unexciting day come alive for him. When he calls you, you should always have some word ready for him to make him glad that he called. If you can't think of anything positive off the cuff, give him an uplifting Scripture. It will be like a glass of cool water refreshing his soul. Your words should minister to him on three levels: mentally, emotionally, and spiritually.

Next, salt is a preservative that keeps food from spoiling. Your words should be used as a preservative to build, maintain, and solidify the foundation of your friendship or romance. Proverbs 14:1 says, "The wise woman builds her house, but with her hands the foolish woman tears hers down." The same can be said of words. Male egos are fragile; they bruise easily, and their recovery time is much longer than that of a woman's. So don't abuse your power. Preserve that relationship!

Salt can also melt snow. Your words should melt his heart and his defenses, leaving the road clear for a smooth drive to your love destination.

Lastly, salt is used in everything imaginable because of its ability to hold things together. Did you know that salt is even used in the concrete they pour to pave streets? It keeps the cement from crumbling and cracking. Make sure your words are constructive and not destructive. Remember, for every negative thing you have to say, there's a woman out there just waiting to whisper sweet somethings in your man's ear and take him off your hands! So be gracious. "Pleasant words are a honeycomb, sweet to the soul and healing to the bones" (Proverbs 16:24 NIV). I am amazed at all the things women are willing to do on a surface level for men—everything from sleeping with them to buying them expensive gifts. But these same women completely ignore the opportunity they have to minister deeply to the inner man. This is a serious mistake!

Don't Buy Him Expensive Gifts

A little sidebar about buying gifts for men—*don't*. Be a gift, don't *give* a gift. Until after he's given you one, that is. And then make your gift something small and thoughtful that will bring a smile to his face. Do not, I repeat, *do not* give him expensive gifts. They most likely will not be taken in the spirit in which they were given. A costly gift will be taken as a hint that he should reciprocate in like expensive manner. Worse yet, he'll feel pressured to respond to you even though his feelings for you aren't as deep as your feelings for him, and he will either use you or flee. I recall a friend of mine who knew someone who worked at a golf club company. She was able to get a free set of golf clubs, and she gave them to a man she liked. I flinched as she told me what she had done. I could read the end of the book already! Sure enough, he began acting more interested than he had been previously, but eventually he broke it off with her and married someone else. Can you imagine how she felt even though she didn't pay for the clubs? She paid with something even more costly—her heart.

Oh, but the story doesn't end there! I happened to visit another friend of mine, all the way across the country, some time later. While flipping through one of her photo albums, I saw a picture of this same man. I commented, "I didn't know you knew him. I have a friend who was crazy about this guy. She sent him a pair of golf clubs!" To which my friend replied, "Girl, I was there the day he received them. You know what he said? 'I don't want a woman who chases after me. I want to do the chasing!' I didn't know the girl, but I sure felt sorry for her." Not as sorry as I felt, I thought to myself. My friend was a beautiful sister with only the best of innocent intentions. I'm sure she felt it was all right to send him this gift since it wasn't really costing her anything financially. But in the end I think the experience was more expensive than she anticipated or imagined.

Be a Gift

Believe me when I say that men don't care about presents as much as we do. They are simply looking for a woman who will help them be a better man. A man who feels effective in life is a happy camper. This is a man who will pick flowers along the way and bring them home to you. If "man shall not live by bread alone, but by every word that proceeds from the mouth of God" (Matthew 4:4 NKJV), how much more do your words affect those in your world now that the spirit of God dwells in you?

If a shout could bring down the walls of Jericho and by the words "Let there be..." the world was fashioned, just think what your words can produce in the life of a man. *Principles* women understand and know that their words have power! They know that they are spirit and they are life. They look past what they see to what can be in Christ, and they "[call] things that are not as though they were," into the lives of their loved ones (Romans 4:17 NIV). A *Principles* woman's presence in the life of a man becomes pivotal in the course of his circumstances.

Now, I'm not encouraging you to walk in denial of major problem areas. You should take these to God in prayer. Wait for His leading on how to either "speak the truth in love" (see Ephesians 4:15), be silent and allow Him to move in the person's life, or remove yourself from the situation. No matter what the outcome, make it your mission to be a woman who encourages, lifts, inspires, and motivates the man in your life and everyone else you meet to be their God-ordained best. Now, that's some serious marinade that's bound to make all of your relationships juicy and flavorful!

Prayer

Heavenly Father, I release my conversation to You. I ask that the Holy Spirit guide my thoughts and guard my tongue. Help me to always be a vessel for Your glory. Help me to always edify, uplift, refresh, and inspire those around me. Give me a spirit that is yielded to You completely. Fill my mouth with good things— things that give life, promote truth, and spread love. Let me be a fountain that brings forth blessings and not curses. Use me as Your instrument of grace, in Jesus' Name. Amen.

Principle #9

Know How to Take Advice

No one comes into the world knowing everything there is to know about relationships. In fact, I think we look more like empty computers when we first arrive on planet earth. No programs have been installed. All we have is the capacity to record and store all the information we receive. The operative word here is *all*. Right or wrong, that data is stored based on our observances, and that's what makes up our programming. And we print out what we retain. Sometimes this is a good thing, sometimes it's not.

I know I drove my girlfriend Denise crazy. I would call her, tell her what was going on with the man presently in my life and tell her exactly what I was going to do about the situation. She would always say the same thing: "Don't do it." I would justify why I should and stomp off in defiance to carry out my resolve. After the smoke cleared I would crawl back to her and say, "Okay, I did what you told me not to do. Now everything is really a mess—how do I fix it?" She would look at me shake her head and laugh as if to say, "You silly goose." After several trips around the same mountain I concluded that doing it "my way" wasn't conducive to getting the response I wanted. It was time to switch my disk, so to speak, and get some new information in my hard drive before I crashed.

Some programming needs to be deleted and new information needs to be filed. This is where the trouble begins! Most of us prefer to continue careening down the path of destructive patterns in relationships—printing out bad data, if you will—and go out in a blaze of glory singing, "I Did It My Way."

Let me ask you a question. What did doing it your way profit you? Are you getting anywhere? The truth is, no one has to like you the way you are. It's a choice. Therefore, if something is wrong and it's been brought to your attention, submit it to the Holy Spirit and get on with fixing it. On the flip side, if you find yourself caught in a pattern of failing relationships but no one has told you anything, ask the Lord. He'll be happy to show you what the problem is. You don't have a personal monopoly on mistakes. Everyone makes them, so don't be ashamed to admit that you messed up. Rejoice that the truth has been revealed. Now you can do something about it! "You shall know the truth, and the truth shall make you free" (John 8:32 NKJV). Or, as they say in Urbanese, "The truth is the light."

Listen to Your Mentors

I find it interesting that the Bible tells older women to be teachers of good things "that they may teach the young women to be sober, to love their husbands, to love their children. To be discreet, chaste, keepers at home, good, obedient to their own husbands, that the word of God be not blasphemed" (Titus 2:4-5 KJV). So listen to your mentors! Single women really do need an education when it comes to this whole relationship thing. As my friend P. Bunny Wilson so aptly says in her book *The Master's Degree*, "Who taught you to be married?" We study in order to prepare ourselves for a career in life, but we fail to study for the lifelong career of marriage and relationships. Speaking of things that make you go hmmm, let's flush this thing out!

Take the story of Ruth. Naomi told Ruth what to do in order to win the heart of Boaz. Ruth didn't put her hand on her hip and tell her mother-in-law, "Now, look, I've been married before! You don't need to tell me what to do. I know a thing or two about men, you know. I didn't have any trouble getting your son's attention, did I? This is my personal business so stay out of it!" It's a good thing Ruth didn't respond that way. She listened and followed Naomi's advice without giving her mother-in-law any lip. Her reward for listening to good advice? A very kind, very rich husband. Not to mention that she ended up contributing to the lineage of Jesus Christ!

Ask Someone Who's Been There

For more reasons to take good advice, turn to the second chapter in the book of Esther. You'll find something very interesting in the story of how she was chosen to be queen. Each woman who had been gathered from around the kingdom to audition for the part of the future queen was able to choose something from the harem to take to the king's palace. Now, let's think about this. If you had never lived in a palace before and had never met the king, how would you know what it takes to please him? Well, why not ask somebody who knew? Just because you've been wearing loud red lipstick outlined with black pencil all your life—and nobody's ever told you it's not exactly your most flattering look—doesn't mean the man you're interested in is going to like it. And he won't tell you it turns him off because he's not interested in hurting your feelings or causing a scene. He'll just move on instead.

Esther played it smart and asked. As woman after woman was sent back by the king, she figured out that whatever these women were doing wasn't working. They were doing what they were used to doing, but it wasn't striking the king's fancy. He wasn't looking for the common; he was looking for something special. Esther knew she didn't have a clue, and didn't even attempt to guess what that something special might be. The story goes on to say that, "When the turn came for Esther to go to the king, she asked for nothing other than what Hegai, the king's eunuch who was in charge of the harem, suggested." Just think what would have happened if Esther had said, "Well, you're just a eunuch! What do you know?" But she knew the eunuch had been around long enough to know what the king liked. "Esther won the favor of everyone who saw her" (Esther 2:15 NIV). The conclusion of the story? "The king was attracted to Esther more than to any of the other women, and she won his favor and approval more than any of the other virgins. So he set a royal crown on her head and made her queen instead of Vashti" (Esther 2:17-18 NIV). *The End*, by God.

Keep Following *The Principles*

The end of part one, that is. Some of us feel that once we've gotten where we want to go, we don't have to listen to anyone anymore. We have a tendency to say, "That's okay, I've got it now. I no longer need your assistance." Not true! Things happen and life takes unexpected twists and turns we're not always prepared to handle. In part two we find Esther, a Jewish lady married to a Babylonian king, in a volatile situation. The Jews, captives in the Babylonian empire, weren't exactly the crème de la crème of society. Her uncle Mordecai had instructed Esther not to expose her identity. Ah, but here the plot thickens! A plot to annihilate the Jews is exposed, and guess who's the only hope to saving them? That's right, Esther! Mordecai then tells her she has been brought to her position for "such a time as this"!

Esther wisely rose to the occasion as only a *Principles* woman could do. Instead of panicking and doing something irrational, she fasted and prayed for three days to seek God's advice on the matter. Then she went to the king and invited him and the perpetrator to dinner. When, after dessert, he asked her what she wanted, she merely invited him to join her for dinner again. She wanted him good and satisfied before she broached the subject!

Again the king came to dinner and asked her what she wanted. He told her she could have it, up to half the kingdom! Now that would have been enough to set some of us off and running in pursuit of our own interests. After all, why worry about the rest of the people when you're the queen? But Esther humbled herself and told him she didn't really want to bother him, but the lives of her people were in danger. How's that for handling a scary predicament with finesse and grace? And because of her manner, the king quickly jumped to her defense and nipped the whole awful plot in the bud. Ah, the virtues of following sage advice!

The advice God gave Esther is advice we'd all do well to follow when we're in a place of distress or discontentment. Esther found a way to serve the person who could do something about her situation. As she humbled herself, the king's heart softened and he attended to her needs. And even then she didn't jump ahead of herself. She related her fears without accusing, apologized for any inconvenience this problem would cause him, and asked for his help. Notice she *asked*, she didn't demand. No one is ever obligated to do anything about your situation, but the way you share your need certainly will affect the response you get!

On the flip side of this is an example of someone who didn't follow advice—a guy named Samson. Samson was living proof of the saying "A hard head makes a soft butt," though his disobedience actually cost him a whole lot more. His parents tried to discourage him from marrying a Philistine woman, but he'd already made up his mind. So off he went heading for certain disaster! You can read about it in Judges chapter fourteen. The bottom line is this: not listening to advice cost Samson dearly. And because he refused to learn that lesson, a chain of unwise decisions had been started that would eventually cost him his life.

Two Kinds of Advice

Now it's important to understand there's good advice and bad advice. The secret to taking advice is actually quite plain and simple. Take advice from someone who's been successful at accomplishing what you want to accomplish. Because we're focused on relationships here, find someone who has a successful marriage or relationship and use that person as a source for sound counsel. Do not sit around with a bunch of your girlfriends who aren't having success with men and expect to come away with healthy words of wisdom! What is their track record? Think about it. Plus remember that misery loves company. Sometimes the best of intentions are colored with something else, like a nice, mild shade of green envy! As unconscious as it may be, you don't need its devastating ability at work in your life.

Proverbs 12:15 says, "The way of a fool is right in his own eyes, but he who heeds counsel is wise" (NKJV). Are you really serious about being prepared for love? Take counsel among the successful, submit your findings to God, and allow the Holy Spirit to give you personalized instructions for your situation. When in doubt do nothing. But when you hear from the throne room and your spirit is settled, do as it says on a box of hair perm: *Follow directions carefully to avoid hair breakage, scalp irritation, and eye injury.* In other words, don't decide you know what you're doing and end up with a mess on your hands! It's too late in the day to deliberately open ourselves up to broken hearts, irritated souls, and damaged perceptions. That's not God's will for our lives. So before we even get involved with any man let's ask God, "What's the deal, Lord? Should I let this one pass or proceed forward?" The quickest way to end a depressing drama is to not let it begin. Take my advice!

Prayer

Lord, give me ears that hear and obey what the Spirit says. Help me to value and take sound counsel to heart. Give me a heart to trust that You will always guide me in the way that is best for me. Let my hope rest in You, knowing that you know the deep and hidden desires of my soul and will deliver me at the appropriate time. Let my knowledge of Your promises drown out the cries of my flesh for immediate gratification. Speak to my heart, Lord. Show me the way I should take, in Jesus' Name. Amen.

Principle #10

Learn How to Dress

*I*t's really interesting to me how men and women see things differently. Have you ever been in a shop, tried on something, and asked the salesgirl what she thought? After hearing her opinion on how wonderful that dress or pair of shoes that you're considering looks on you, you then turned and asked a male friend his opinion. To your surprise, he didn't like it at all! This tells me that there is a schism between what men find attractive and what women *think* men find attractive. The bottom line is, they enjoy looking at other women who dress in a manner that exposes all their assets. BUT, they don't like *their* woman dressing like that. They feel that their personal treasure is much better protected beneath modest, but attractive attire.

Why is learning how to dress so important? Because it's the first thing people see when you make an entrance. Your clothes say a lot about you. You can be disregarded or taken seriously based on your appearance. Have you ever walked into an exclusive store looking your best and had everyone flocking to assist you? What happened when you returned to the same store in scruffy casual clothes? The salesgirls either ignored you, or if they did ask you if they could help you, they asked with an entirely different motive. You were highly suspect, not considered the right clientele. Such is life. Looks are important, but what's beneath the surface is even more important. Ever met a person who wasn't anything special on the outside, but they had a way about them that demanded your attention and respect? There you have it!

Dress It Up Inside and Out

So while you're putting your best face forward with a man, don't ignore your inner wardrobe! The Bible pays a lot of attention to clothing, and how we dress—inside *and* out is important to God. He says that husbands will be won over without words by their wives' behavior when they see the purity and reverence of their lives. It goes on to say that "Your beauty should not come from outward adornment, such as braided hair and the wearing of gold jewelry and fine clothes. Instead, it should be that of your inner self, the unfading beauty of a gentle and quiet spirit, which is of great worth in God's sight. For this is the way the holy women of the past who put their hope in God used to make themselves beautiful. They were submissive to their own husbands, like Sarah, who obeyed Abraham and called him her master. You are her daughters if you do what is right and do not give way to fear" (1 Peter 3:3-6 NIV).

Now I find this very interesting. *What does fear have to do with marring beauty?* I asked myself, and then it hit me. Fear makes you a control freak, which is most unattractive! Do you know when you look most beautiful to a man? When you're not giving him a hard time. When he says, "Let me handle it," and you say, "Okay"—and actually behave as if you trust him to handle it. Well—his heart beats a little faster at the look of complete trust and confidence in him upon your face. And you can have confidence in him because you trust his ability to hear from God and be obedient. You trust God to get his attention and make him do the right thing! This will keep you looking knock-down, drag-out gorgeous in his eyes long after the laugh lines, crow's feet, extra weight, and gray hairs appear. Remember, these *inner* qualities are the secret to unfading beauty.

The Bible makes many references to garments of salvation, garments of praise, and robes of righteousness...you see where this is heading! Fear tells you that you have to add another layer of makeup, buy more expensive accessories, and wear tighter, skimpier clothing. Fear whispers that you have to compete with all the other cuties out there, and that you don't measure up. Perhaps you should add some more hair (more than you need). Do something more noticeable to yourself.

I recall a very funny scene in a movie where two people who had met in a bar decided to retire to the woman's home to become more intimate. Being kind of innocent, the guy decided he should confess that one of his physical attributes did not really live up to his boasting. The woman was so relieved to hear this that she too began to confess that her hair wasn't real as she pulled off her wig to reveal a bald pate with one single curl, her eyes weren't real as she popped out her colored lens, and she had padded her bra and her girdle. Why even one of her legs wasn't real, she excitedly revealed as she threw her prosthesis across the room! Well, the man was horrified and fled. The scene ended with her hopping across the room shouting, "Don't make me have to hop after you!" It was hysterical, but it proves my point in an exaggerated way.

Remember, a stop sign only holds a driver's attention long enough for the traffic to clear so that he can make his way across the street. Don't be a temporary attraction. Go for beauty secrets that last!

Because "man looks at the outward appearance, but the LORD looks on the heart," it's safe to assume that a godly man—and that is the type of man you really want—is of the same mindset. He might initially be moved by what he sees, but eventually he's going to look past that and begin checking out your spirit (see Samuel 16:7).

So dress it up girl! "What should I wear?" is the first question we ask as we dash off to tell a friend about our hot date. Let me make a few wardrobe suggestions.

Wear the Right Color

First of all, the color red is always stunning. Red is the color of redemption, not to be confused with scarlet or crimson. It's important to wear true red, which is most complimentary to your spiritual complexion. And white undergarments are a must. White is the color of purity. These things should be easy to find because God promises that though our sins be as scarlet he will make us white as snow, though they be red like crimson, they shall be as wool (see Isaiah 1:18). So if you're wearing the wrong shade, it's not too late to make an exchange.

Get Some Good Footwear

Now let's work on those feet, girl! According to God's fashion guide, "How beautiful on the mountains are the feet of those who bring good news, who proclaim peace, who bring good tidings, who proclaim salvation" (Isaiah 52:7 NIV). If your conversation is always uplifting and you're someone who brings peace where there is anxiety and upheaval, who always has a word to encourage, to exhort, to liberate the mind and set the spirit free, that man—*everyone* for that matter—will be happy to see you coming. The mountains are the places in life where one must exert energy to keep climbing, so good news is always welcome. Therefore, your feet need to be "fitted with the readiness that comes from the gospel of peace" (Ephesians 6:15 NIV). Move over, Stuart Weitzman, these shoes are definitely made for walking!

Complete the Outfit

Well, we can't have you walking around in just shoes, can we? So what else should you wear? Let's start by covering your breast with righteousness. "When a [woman's] ways please the LORD, he makes even [her] enemies to be at peace with [her]" (Proverbs 16:7 NKJV). If a mere dress could do that, stores wouldn't be able to keep it in stock. Everyone would want one!

Now cinch in that waist with the belt of truth. Not your personal truth, God's truth. You've probably learned the same thing I've learned. Man's opinion is worth approximately two cents, but God's word is priceless. It is a lamp unto our feet. It illuminates our path and leads us to make the right decisions. When we are able to offer others in our life real solutions based on God's supreme knowledge, it's a beautiful thing. A good belt pulls your entire outfit together and keeps it from falling down (remember my pantyhose incident? You do not want that to happen in public!).

And now for the accessories! I have a hat fetish. How about you? I prefer salvation berets, trimmed with fur, of course. When salvation crowns your head, it affects your mindset. It rearranges your priorities and puts them in divine order. This will affect every area of your life, including how you handle relationships. But we're not done yet! The sword of the Spirit and the shield of faith are fabulous accessories that definitely make a power statement. Wrap yourself in the zeal of God as a cloak and you, my dear, will be a show-stopper! Now that's an outfit!

One look at you and the man in your life will proclaim, "From Zion, perfect in beauty, God shines forth" (Psalm 50:2 NIV). That's the real beauty of holiness. Wear it well!

Prayer

Dear Lord, dress me in the beauty of Your holiness. Let me never rely on the temporary outer adorning that the world sees as attractiveness, but on the quiet beauty of a yielded life to You. Let Your glory rest on me as I walk obediently before You. As my ways please You, let them also please those around me. Help me to be a blessing in all of my relationships, and let my beauty be the reflection of You in all that I do, in Jesus' Name. Amen.

Master the Art of Cooking

I'm going to take my time with this one because every good cook knows it's best to bring your dish to a slow boil. Another good tip is that when something's boiling, you need to be careful about how you remove the lid from the pot. When removed in haste, the steam from what's in the pot can burn your hand badly. And if you've ever had a steam burn you know it's extremely painful. It gets under your skin and the sting lingers for quite some time. Kind of like what happens when we venture into the realm of physical intimacy outside the boundaries of marriage. No wonder the Shulamite woman said, "Promise me...not to awaken [arouse or stir up] love until the time is right" (Song of Songs 2:7 NLT).

Yeah, girl, it's time to talk about our favorite subject—sex. Now what is sex exactly? Sex is worship. Did you know that? It's important to know what we are dealing with here because this is an area that in a lot of respects is still taboo. Because they don't talk about it, people experiment and use sex for all the wrong reasons. Let's get down to basics and build from there. Everything in the earthly realm has a parallel in the spirit realm. Marriage is the earthly parallel of our union with the Bridegroom, Jesus Christ Himself, in eternity. It is also the reflection of kingdom living. Sex is the earthly parallel of the oneness we will experience when we finally join with Him. The orgasm is the earthly parallel of the ecstasy we will feel *throughout eternity* from that union! Wow! Can you just imagine? That's why we'll need glorified bodies. No human body would be able to contain such a powerful sensation for such a sustained amount of time! But God has chosen to allow us to experience just a smidgen of it here on earth so that we'll have something to look forward to.

When we celebrate God and move from high praise into deep worship, something deep within us is stirred. It's an indescribable feeling that fills our souls, bubbles up, and pours forth from our very being. There's nothing that comes close to it, nothing except sex. It's that same emptying out of self. This is the epitome of being a living sacrifice, giving all that you are and all that you have to the object of your affections. There is no room for pretense; you are naked with no distractions, nothing between the two of you—this is as real as you'll ever get with another person. And when the celebration subsides you find yourself spent but satisfied. It is a glorious thing—in the right context.

Know How to Worship

But *Principles* women need to know and understand that there is a right way to worship and a wrong way to worship. Although God loves worship, there is a type of worship that he finds unacceptable. Cain found that out after He gave a sacrifice that was not pleasing to God. Obviously he and his brother Abel had been instructed on what God expected because Abel gave the right sacrifice. Upon being corrected by God, Cain got an attitude. God continued to gently prod him by saying, "Why are you so angry?... Why do you look so dejected? You will be accepted if you respond in the right way. But if you refuse to respond correctly, then watch out! Sin is waiting to attack and destroy you, and you must subdue it" (Genesis 4:6-7 NLT). But Cain wanted to do what he wanted to do. That's like having a friend ask you what you want for your birthday. You tell her and she decides to get you something else that she wants you to have instead. Never mind that's not what you wanted. Obviously you didn't know what was good for you! No one likes to have their needs ignored that way. But Cain not only ignored God's request, he went a step further. Out of jealousy he killed his brother. Wrong worship not only sets us up for rejection and destroys relationships, it hurts other people!

Then there's the story of the priests Nadab and Abihu who disobeyed the Lord by burning a different kind of fire before Him than what He had commanded. "So fire blazed forth from the LORD's presence and burned them up, and they died there before the LORD" (Leviticus 10:2 NLT). Ever been burned in a relationship? Ever found out far too late that you've been consumed in a relationship you were having all by yourself? You gave your all, which the other party gladly received, but left out one minor detail—he wasn't feeling the same way. It's harder to be discerning of this fact if you've walked out from under the protective umbrella of following God's rules for relationships. Every time you sleep with someone and the relationship doesn't work out, a part of you dies. Wrong worship can hurt you, disfigure your heart, and kill your spirit.

Now let's look at a few stories from God's word that directly deal with sex—the first from 2 Samuel, chapter 13. Amnon, who was lovesick over his half sister, Tamar took some bad advice from his cousin Jonadeb. He was madly in love with Tamar to the point of obsession. Actually to the point of depression. He felt he would never be able to do anything about it.

That's when Jonadeb stepped in and suggested to Amnon that he should pretend to be ill, then get daddy David's permission to have Tamar come and cook for him. When Tamar came to Amnon's room, he raped her even though she pleaded with him and even suggested they ask the king if they could be married. But her words fell on deaf ears. After he had taken her, the Bible says he hated her with an intense hatred. As a matter of fact, he hated her more than he had "loved her." He commanded his servants to throw "this woman" out! She went from being the beautiful Tamar to "this woman." Even then, she asked him to redeem the situation. According to levitical law, if a man raped a virgin who was not engaged he was to pay her family fifty shekels of silver, marry her, and never divorce her. But Amnon wasn't interested in marrying Tamar. Why? Because he had never been "in love" with her. He was simply "in lust" with her. The story ends sadly with Tamar living out the rest of her life in desolation in her brother Absalom's house. Absalom later killed Amnon to avenge his sister's lot in life.

This story has shades of a modern-day exchange. Poor Tamar! All she wanted to do was get married. But that's obviously not where Amnon's head was. He just wanted to have a good time and fulfill the lust of his flesh. Many women today have been deceived into thinking that giving themselves totally to a man will secure a commitment from him. But men are interesting creatures! They will try you and then be disappointed when you give in, even though they enjoyed taking advantage of the situation. The enemy then comes along and convinces them that you're manipulating them into an obligation. They resent it and flee. Same old story, even way back then.

What was the fruit of this whole experience? The spiritual death of Absalom, who fell into sin and killed his own brother. The physical death of Amnon. The death of Tamar's desirability. No one wanted to marry her now that she was no longer a virgin. Perhaps today a woman is not so heavily condemned for not being a virgin, but, when she is rejected after being intimate with a man she tends to question her own desirability. Her self-esteem suffers as she tries to figure out, "What's wrong with me? I thought he really liked me. What happened?"

I'll tell you what happened. The woman stepped down from her power base. God gave woman the gift of desirability to get man's attention. He gave man the gift of testosterone so that he would feel a need for woman and make a commitment. Remember, men are basically independent agents. That's why it took God's prompting to make Adam realize he was alone! He was perfectly content taking care of himself and tending the garden. But once he experienced Eve, that was it! He didn't even let sin separate them—he chose Eve over close fellowship with God.

You're Worth a Fortune

When you turn over the house without having him sign the contract, he never feels the need to buy it. Why should he, when he can move in and make himself comfortable for free? When you have relinquished your power and lessened your worth your spirit man knows it and mourns. Your love should be expensive, like the pearl of great price. Chew on this: the man who truly loves you will be willing to pay the price for you, like the merchant "who, when he had found one pearl of great price, went and sold all that he had, and bought it" (Matthew 13:46 KJV). He'll sell worldly ideas about sex before marriage, other women he's kept on reserve…you name it, he'll get rid of it, in order to be in position to win you! Jesus paid the price to redeem you. How much more should a mortal man be willing to pay to possess your love?

Now I heard some of you hard-headed, thoroughly-modern Millies muttering under your breath. "Oh, *puh-leeze!* Aren't you stretching it, Michelle? What about all of the people who have sex and still make a commitment? Just go to any breakfast joint on the weekends and you'll see all the people who slept together the night before still together, still having a good time." You're right, and I've got something to say about that.

Let's take a look at Genesis chapter 34. Here we have Dinah, Jacob's only daughter, walking along minding her own business. Enter the local prince, Shechem. He sees her, decides that she is a tempting morsel, and, as the Bible puts it, he "saw her, he took her, and raped her" (verse 2 NLT). Three steps to the deed, so it was calculated. The King James Version goes on to say, "And his soul clave unto Dinah the daughter of Jacob, and he loved the damsel, and spake kindly unto the damsel." He even talked to his father about it. "'Get this girl for me,' he demanded, 'I want to marry her.'" So then Shechem's father went to Jacob saying, "The soul of my son Shechem longeth for your daughter: I pray you give her him to wife" (NLT). That seems honorable enough, but what was his love based on? He didn't know her. This is where lust arrives disguised as love. What it really is beneath the feelings of passion is a "soul tie."

God created sex not only as worship, but as glue to bind two people together. This was the thing that would make them work out their differences when they wanted to leave each other. He literally intended to "tie" the two souls together so that the two become one (see Genesis 2:24). This is why Satan does not like "right worship." He constantly works to pervert it. He works overtime to separate couples and tempt singles. I once heard a minister say, "Married people have the license to operate their sex drive and they don't even want to get in the car, while the singles are saying, 'Can we borrow your driver's license?' The singles are burning and the married people are cold." Now do you see the trick of the enemy?

Anyway, back to Dinah and Shechem. Shechem took his father and went to ask for Dinah's hand in marriage. Her brothers agreed, on the condition that Shechem and the rest of the men of their village consented to be circumcised. Shechem and his father, too happy to comply with their request, scurried off to convince the rest of the region's men to go along with their wishes. They told the men that this could be a very lucrative alliance on everyone's part because Jacob's family was very wealthy. Their argument worked, and all the men went along with the plan. On the third day, when all the men were healing, Dinah's brothers raided the place, took Dinah from Shechem's house, and seized everything living—women, children, flocks...I mean *everything!* This greatly distressed Jacob. He feared retaliation from their neighbors, so his family packed up and left the area immediately. The brothers, on the other hand, were unrepentant because they felt their sister had been treated like a prostitute.

Poor Dinah's hopes for a husband were now dashed as well, and her family was forced to move like vagabonds because of all the ruckus that had been raised on her behalf. What do we get out of this? Yes, some men are willing to commit after they have slept with you, but at what cost? By what motivation? Are you ever really sure? Situations like these usually open the door for offense on some level, cause irreparable rifts in communication, annihilate trust, and leave room for emotional uncertainty and the death of future security.

"But Michelle," you say, "lots of people have sex while they're courting, get married, and live happily ever after. I'm still not convinced that this is such a big deal. And my brothers love me, but I sure can't picture them murdering a whole city on my behalf!" Again, you're absolutely right. So let's talk about David and Bathsheba. Here we have David, the illustrious king of Israel, apple of God's eye, in 2 Samuel chapter 11. The Bible says he was taking a stroll on the roof of his palace when he noticed a woman of unusual beauty. He appointed someone to find out who she was, sent for her, and when she came to the palace he slept with her. (I find it interesting that all these kings got the first two steps of courtship right, then blew it on the third. They noticed, they approached, and then they went overboard. Perhaps this comes from being used to having whatever they wanted. Kinda like a lot of men today!) Bathsheba was then sent back to her home. After all, David couldn't very well get away with keeping a married woman in the palace now, could he? But this is where a little monkey wrench gets thrown into this tidy little encounter. Bathsheba gets pregnant and sends word to David.

David's first response was not to claim responsibility. *No-o-o!* He sends for Uriah to come home so that Uriah can sleep with his wife and pass the baby off as his own. So you tell me, whose best interests did David have at heart? Was he in love or in passing lust at this point? Well, his pitiful attempt to slither out of the mess failed because Uriah refused to take pleasure in his wife while his partners were still at war fighting. David then decided to take desperate measures. He saw a serious storm brewing if he didn't do something right away. So he sent Uriah back to the battle and promptly had him killed.

David then married Bathsheba. But God was not amused. Nathan the prophet was sent to call David on the carpet. The baby that had been conceived died, and David knew that he had no defense against God's judgment.

Yes, the story does end with David really falling in love with Bathsheba. I'm sure the trial they endured brought them closer together than ever. She had another son, the infamous Solomon, and remained close to David until his death. But the repercussions from their union were devastating. Satan had a field day with the family.

It was after these events that David's son Amnon raped his daughter Tamar. I'm sure David's son Absalom was upset with his father for not punishing Amnon for his actions, and that this gave birth to his bitterness against his father. The Bible simply states that when David heard of the events he became very angry. I am of the opinion that David was still under condemnation about his earlier fall from grace and did not feel he could in good conscience confront his son. He couldn't bear to risk having accusations hurled back into his face. He knew the palace gossip mill had enjoyed discussing his private little scandal. So Absalom took the matter into his own hands and killed Amnon, then went on to lead a revolt against David and sleep with his father's wives on the palace rooftop in full view of all of Israel. Ironic, isn't it? The original place of sin for David became the place of his disgrace.

What happened here? God says He will show His "unfailing love to many thousands by forgiving every kind of sin and rebellion. Even so I do not leave sin unpunished, but I punish the children for the sins of their parents to the third and fourth generation" (Exodus 34:7 NLT). In other words, David's actions released a generational curse on his children. This lust problem went on and on. David's other son, Abinadeb, asked for one of his father's concubines, and Solomon ended up sleeping with a thousand women and spending his last years in despair. So while you're having a good time, think about the destiny of your children and how your actions will affect them. All of that trouble for a little roll in the hay. Was it really worth it? I think not. Thank God He is able to salvage all things. He maintained the lineage of Christ through this family in spite of all the madness! But again at a high and painful cost that could have been avoided.

Keep Your Eyes Open

Of course, this portfolio of promiscuity would not be complete without Samson. Quick down and dirty, lust blinded Samson to all the obvious warning signs. Come on, if you told someone a secret and found out that he had betrayed you, would you be quick to give him any more information? Yet Samson, blinded by his hormones, fell into that trap not once but twice with two Philistine women. The last, Delilah, cost him his life. The wrong kind of worship blinds us and robs us of discernment. We're not able to see the other person as they truly are, and before we know it we sail blissfully into a trap. Even if we see it coming, it's difficult for us to remove ourselves from the situation because of that little thing called a soul tie. It's hard to break away because the soul tie was not designed to be broken. It's like ripping a patch out of your spirit. Tell me, how many tears can your spirit take and still retain any hope of wholeness?

The Perfect Love Recipe

This is why it's important to keep a lid on the love pot. Stick to God's recipe for perfect, healthy love. Love is fragile like a soufflé.

If you stick it in the microwave and heat it up too fast, it will explode. If you put it in the oven and open the door too soon, it will fall flat and be ruined. But when cooked properly, it rises and becomes a tasty delight for those who partake of it.

You haven't been waiting all this time simply to wind up with a man who can't wait for the fullness of your love. You are waiting for a Boaz. When Boaz spotted Ruth his first move was to observe her and provide for her. When he found her sleeping at his feet on the threshing floor, he covered her up and sent her home early before anyone could see her leaving his place. He protected her reputation. And then he went and paid the price he needed to pay to marry her. That's what you want. You will never doubt that man's love for you because you will know that he was willing to do whatever it took to have you in his life.

I assume that many of you reading this book are not virgins. But don't despair, there is hope for you! Because you have been born again, you are a virgin in Christ. It's now up to you to keep yourself pure for the man who He has ordained to find you. In the meantime, direct your worship toward God until you are released to worship in fellowship with another. Keep the home fires burning but keep a lid on the love pot!

Prayer

Heavenly Father, I submit my body to You. I ask that Your Holy Spirit rise up in me and equip me to keep myself holy and set apart unto You. Help me to value my body as You value it. Help me to please Your heart over the flesh of man. Quiet the longings of my own flesh and keep me so that I will not sin against You and against my own body. Keep me unto the day when You will smile upon my union with the one who You have chosen for me. I willingly give myself to You as a living sacrifice, that I may prove what is Your good and acceptable will. Help me. Keep me from crawling off the altar. Let the vision of what You have in store for me establish my resolve to wait until that day when it will be permissible to share my love in intimacy with another, in Jesus' Name. Amen.

Principle #12

Know How to Sow

I was flipping through an old poetry journal of mine one day when I found a poem I had written some time back. It said: "I'm lonely, so lonely I don't have to peel an onion to cry, so lonely I've given each wall a name, and though they can't talk back, they listen just the same, so lonely frustration has become my first name, so lonely, that depression is my middle name, and for now I'm gonna wallow in my desperation...after all, I'm lonely. And that's as good an excuse as any for sitting around and feeling sorry for the way my life is going."

Oh, it gets worse! I turned the page and found this little gem: "Mama told me there's an owner for every cloth in the store. Well, I'm ready to be bought. I've been sitting here with the same pretty pattern on my face for a long time and I'm beginning to fade, ya know?"

And how could I have forgotten this classic? "I'm gonna get up and go out lookin' real ugly this mornin'...as ugly as I feel, gonna cop a monstrous attitude and growl at the world...and everyone will say what's wrong with her, and go right on not caring. And no one will contribute to my self-pity or whatever bag I'm into. I'm not really sure myself. I think I'm in limbo at the end of the waiting list." On and on, page after page, an entire section of my journal sounded like this! Poor little me, forsaken in the big old bad world with no one to watch over me, or to kiss the hurt and make it better. I had been destined to the most horrible fate of all—that of being alone. Woe is me, alas and alack.

Needless to say, I was mortified by my torturous ramblings. It dredged up days and nights of single misery. I could almost feel the pain that would tighten my chest back in those days. I remembered going home after work and sitting on the couch, curled up in a corner feeling sorry for myself. All I could do back then was concentrate on how alone I felt, review every failed relationship, and weep. You got it! I was completely self-involved.

Have you ever stood and stared at yourself in the mirror for an endless amount of time? Ever notice that when you do this little exercise, the longer you gaze at your reflection, the more you find wrong with yourself? The more time you spend with yourself, fantasizing about what would make your life perfect and going over the list of everything that's missing from your life, the more lonely you will be. Not only is loneliness the perfect formula for desperation and neediness, but loneliness is also a good man repellent. I think men have a silent alarm inside of them that sounds whenever they come within a two-mile radius of a lonely, needy woman. The moment the alarm goes off, they flee at the speed of light. They don't want the responsibility of furnishing the entertainment or being the filler in your life.

Spread the Love

So what's the antidote for loneliness? It's getting out of self. You've heard the phrase "Spread the love?" Well, that's what you have to do, girl! You've got to get busy. Love those who are available to be loved right now! "Remember this: Whoever sows sparingly will also reap sparingly, and whoever sows generously will also reap generously" (2 Corinthians 9:6 NIV). As you begin to reach out to people around you, that love will come back full circle and begin to fill the empty holes in your life. People call my house "Michelle's Bed and Breakfast," because someone is always visiting, stopping by, or calling me. My life is full of loving people—men, women, and children. That's right, even children!

I decided I was no longer going to leave any open spaces in my life for the enemy to point out and take advantage of. If I wanted children, I would just borrow someone else's. The parents would be happy for the break, and I'd have my child fix. That's how you shut the mouth of the enemy—you fill your life with activity. I got involved in the lives of others. I started taking care of kingdom business. This is what Paul meant when he said, "I say therefore to the unmarried and widows, it is good for them if they abide even as I....The unmarried woman careth for the things of the Lord, that she may be holy both in body and spirit: but she that is married careth for the things of the world, how she may please her husband. And this I speak for your own profit; not that I may cast a snare upon you, but for that which is comely, and that ye may attend upon the Lord without distraction" (1 Corinthians 7:8,34-35 KJV).

I must admit that for a long time Paul's words upset me. I wanted what I wanted out of life *right now!* I had no idea of how to fill my life today until what I wanted came tomorrow. But, in the end, I robbed myself of the joy of fulfillment on another level. My married friends were quick to remind me that nothing would happen in the marriage area of my life until I learned to be happy where I was. They were always quoting, "Not that I speak in respect of want: for I have learned, in whatsoever state I am, therewith to be content" (Philippians 4:11 KJV). I thought Paul sure had a lot of nerve! How could he be so flippant about my desires? But slowly the light came on. As I began to get involved in the needs of others, I forgot about my own needs. I was distracted by service to the Lord, and the pleasure I got from bringing joy and comfort to others filled me with the warmest glow of satisfaction. The pieces of my world began to come together.

The last frontier for me was getting past being upset with God for making me wait so long for children. I was quick to remind him, "My name is not Sarah, okay?" I would sarcastically tell others, "My biological clock is no longer ticking. It's broken." Even though I said it with laughter, there was a pang of pain attached. Well, my problem has been solved. I am now the joyful guardian of two girls from Africa who are attending school in the States! Elsie and Nicole have slowed down the ticking clock as I now face the reality of being a mother. First of all, it is a lot of work! Secondly, it's one of the greatest blessings I can imagine. As I pour my life into the hearts of these two young ladies, the love and the fruit that springs from them is a source of great joy for me. Elsie and Nicole have caused me to grow, and I hope I've caused them to do the same. All I know is that the way they fill a part of me cannot be described with words.

Elsie and Nicole have answered the question in my heart that I know many of you struggle with. Do you want to be a mother? Or do you just want children for the sake of your own ego, or as validation of your womanhood? Well, there are children available to be loved right here, right now. And though you may long for the experience of birthing a child, the real experience of fulfillment lies in pouring yourself into their little lives and seeing what your care produces. Anyone can have a child, but not everyone can raise a little one in a way that will bring honor to God and a blessing to your life. That opportunity exists for you right now, even if you're not married. This is the reward of loving those who are available to be loved!

I also know a lot of single people who feel ignored and overlooked. They feel there isn't a place for them in the family-oriented church. Know what I say to that? Make a name for yourself. Approach leadership, pointing out that they are ignoring Paul's words and aren't making effective use of their single members. Singles can make a powerful contribution to the church, to the families within the church, and to the leadership of the church. Go in armed with ideas and get busy! Too many singles groups meet to do things that last only for an evening. How about becoming more project-oriented? There's something to be said for making effectual contributions in the lives of those who have a need you can fill.

A *Principles* Woman in Love

Something else happens once you get busy sowing. You fall in love with life itself. When a *Principles* woman is in love, suddenly she becomes attractive to everyone around her. There's a special glow that transmits from her. She's smiling. She's not uptight or easily upset. Her mind is on her mission. She doesn't have time to dwell on trivial setbacks. She's open and approachable. This is the best state to be in. Let's face it, you never know who's watching. A Boaz might be checking you out!

One of the things that impressed Boaz was the kindness Ruth exhibited by leaving her own country and customs behind, literally forsaking her heritage to take care of her mother-in-law, Naomi. Boaz saw this as a good quality. And he saw Ruth as good wife material. Can you imagine if he had caught her sulking and feeling sorry for herself, or being flirtatious with every man who passed by? He would have thought, "Hmmph! Typical Moabite woman—no morals, unholy idol worshipper." And that would have been the end of the story. But Ruth chose not to bemoan her lot in life and instead sowed into the life of her mother-in-law. The reward she reaped was the cherished love of a good man.

Even the virtuous woman of Proverbs 31:20 understood the benefits of sowing and reaping. Even though she had a family, "She opens her arms to the poor and extends her hands to the needy." She was not a selfish woman; she saw to the needs of her entire household, including her servants. She was known as a kind woman who gave good advice and faithful words of encouragement to everyone. She was well-received by all because of what she gave. Her life was a rich one, and her husband and children acknowledged her greatness, confessing that they were blessed to have her in their lives.

The long and short of it is that you can sit and focus on that one little lonely patch in your life, or you can see the beauty and endless possibilities of what you can do for others. As you get busy pulling together all the pieces of your life, you'll create a beautiful quilt of fulfillment. That's what sowing is all about. And you know that the true beauty of a quilt is its uniqueness. No two quilts are the same. Each pattern is magnificent in its own right. People are fascinated with the labor of love and the work that went into its creation. Hey, I'm talking about you!

Prayer

Dear Lord, pull me out of self and into Your service. Help me to love those who are available to be loved and blessed by me. Show me those who have needs around me that I can fill. Help me as I give my life away to find a new dimension of honoring You through reaching out to others. Let me be blessed through being a blessing to others. Fill my life, Lord, with Your purposes and Your desires for me. Manifest Your goodness to others through me, and help me to discover the joy of Your salvation as I pour my life out to those around me, in Jesus' Name. Amen.

Principle #13

Get into Gardening

A friend of mine once told me a joke about a guy who got into a cab, shut the door, and suddenly noticed a most horrible smell. He sat in the cab thinking that the cab driver had to be out of his mind not to notice that he was suffering from an acute case of B.O. The man opened the windows and fanned himself, all to no avail. After a while he couldn't take it any longer. He ordered the cab driver to a halt and exited the car. Still muttering under his breath about how anyone could smell that bad and be so oblivious, he walked down the street and entered a building. As he walked into the elevator and the door closed behind him, the same overwhelming smell filled his nostrils. Looking down, he noticed the soles his shoes were covered in dog dung! The object of the lesson? Perhaps it's not always the other person who's the problem. It could be you!

That's right, we're sometimes guilty of having a downright putrid attitude assisted by a whole lot of "stinkin' thinkin'"! When that happens, it's time to dig a hole in the ground and bury that stuff! It makes me think of the time when a guy who admired me sent an arrangement of flowers to my office. I didn't like the guy, but I loved the flowers. They were absolutely beautiful! I scooped them up and set them in the window where they could enjoy the sun. Well, as the day progressed and the sunshine streamed in through my window, a most acrid smell filled my office! It actually gave me a headache. I finally figured out the smell was coming from the flowers—they were onion flowers! Needless to say, I hurried up and got that flower arrangement out of my office. My coworkers thought it was hilarious, but those onion flowers didn't help my like-meter go up. Poor guy, he didn't have a clue!

What am I getting at? Most of us who have had a hard time with relationships and find ourselves going through the revolving door of courtship are pretty banged up inside. We still look pretty on the outside, but when the sun rises and heat gets applied to our hearts, all those past problems resurface in the form of a funky attitude. And a funky attitude usually sets you up as a victim in your next relationship. This is why I'm not an advocate of running from relationship to relationship. Let's face it, you only need one mate. After being repeatedly hurt and abused, you won't need a mate—you'll need a specialist who can deal with all your residual stuff. Contrary to popular belief, there are plenty of mates around but good specialists are hard to find!

Enlist a Master Gardener

So what does it take to make an attitude adjustment? It takes the touch of a master horticulturist. A gardener, honey, a gardener. It takes a little digging. You know, some soul searching. Then you have to get rid of all the weeds and stones that choke out and hinder productive new growth. Next you must plant a seed. You need to keep the hope of a new beginning alive. Now cover the seed with earth, keeping your dream in a secret place—preferably in God's hands. Water that seed. Cry if you must. Whatever it takes to cleanse and rinse the heart, do it and remember: "Those who sow in tears will reap with songs of joy. [She] who goes out weeping, carrying seed to sow, will return with songs of joy, carrying sheaves with [her]" (Psalms 126:5,6). The reward of good gardening is a bountiful harvest. You will not leave the field empty-handed.

But "those who plow evil and those who sow trouble reap it" (Job 4:8 NIV). That's what I call bad gardening. What is bad gardening when it comes to the affairs of the heart? It's sowing seeds that promote man-repelling attitudes. Seeds of rejection, anger, bitterness, hatred, and vengeance. And oh, the withered flowers that grow from this crop! Selfishness, which we justify as protecting our emotions. Insecurity, the voice that accuses before there is a reason. Neediness, that screams things like, "Where have you been? What took you so long to call? You never have time for me! You don't really love me!" You know, all the stuff that makes men want to get away from you as quickly as possible.

Insecurity and neediness are part of the same species of plant, and they give off other shoots called idolatry, immorality, and witchcraft. The plant of idolatry turns your desire for a man into an all-consuming passion, even to the point of compromising your standards. The plant of immorality produces sex outside of marriage, adultery, lascivious behavior, and dressing in an attention-getting way that overtly shows off your wares and assets. Whew! That's some stinky bouquet! Add a touch of witchcraft, which is merely the manipulation of enticing someone to do things they're not inclined to do, and you've got a heartbreak waiting to happen. These things are grievous to the spirit because they are works of the flesh. These are relationship-killing weeds. Get rid of them, quick!

It's time to plant a new crop. It's time for the fruit of the spirit to come bursting through the soil of your heart. No matter what, make your aim "love, joy, peace, patience, kindness, goodness, faithfulness, gentleness and self-control" (Galatians 5:22 NIV). The only way to grow this kind of lush fruit is to tuck your heart away in a dark, secret place—the palm of God Himself. Remember, "He that dwelleth in the secret place of the most High shall abide under the shadow of the Almighty" (Psalm 91:1 KJV). This is where the foliage grows thickest and richest, where the sun can't scorch it and the earth retains its moisture, releasing all kinds of good vitamins into the roots of the plant. God wants to keep our hearts like that. But unfortunately we often don't let Him!

Keep Your Heart Safe

The moment we meet a man, we snatch our heart out of God's hand, toss it at this new guy we've gotten all excited about, and say,

"Here!" Small wonder the poor little thing is so banged up. I think it's time to get a clue, don't you? How about trying this approach— you meet man, he's *re-e-al* cute, you like him. Your little heart is all aflutter, revving up to leap out of your chest and at the poor unsuspecting guy. Place your hand over your heart, whisper to it, "Calm down," and put it back in its secret place. And then say this: "God, I think I really like this one. What do you know about him? What is the purpose of his being in my life? Is he the one for me? Should I proceed, or should I not waste my time on him?" This gets rid of many needless weeds!

Now you're at a crucial turning point. If God says no, please listen to Him. Do not proceed and hope that He will change His mind, because He won't! And if you feel that He's given you the go-ahead sign, this doesn't give you free rein to break all of the preceding principles. You must adhere to them more closely than ever!

So many women have made the mistake of running up to some man and telling him that the Lord told her he was to be her husband. This one little sentence has caused more heartbreak and shattered spirits in church circles than you can imagine as the man fled and married someone else. My question to these women is, "Girlfriend, if God let you in on the secret, don't you think He'd let that man know too?"

Remember when the angel told Mary she was going to bear the Son of God? The angel also went to Joseph to let him know what was going on. Ladies, follow the example of Mary! The Bible says, "Mary treasured up all these things and pondered them in her heart" (Luke 2:19 NIV). Ecclesiastes 3:7 says, "There is a time to speak and a time to keep silent." Now is one of those times, because after that man has heard from you it will be difficult for him to hear the Holy Spirit. Why? Because in his mind, the Holy Spirit will now sound like you!

This is where trusting God comes in. If He said it, it will bear witness in that man's heart and come to pass. If He didn't say it, you won't feel embarrassed and hurt. You'll be able to admit that the voice you thought you heard was the longing of your own desire, and you'll be able to release it. Did you know that a lot of pain is birthed out of shame? Be willing to confess that you made a mistake in discernment and let it go so that you can receive the one God really has for you. This little trick of Satan has kept many a woman in bondage for years, including me! Yes, me. I spent five years waiting for a man I believed God told me was my husband. At the end of the whole devastating experience I stood humiliated before everyone who had tried to gently share their doubts with me. And I had to admit that my own desires and plea bargains with God had led me into deception. This is what happens when we decide to choose our own husbands or grow impatient with God's timing. But *Principles* women who "mind their own business" and "get a life" don't usually trip over this weed. They're too busy collecting fruit!

Make Way for Delicious Fruit

So get rid of those rotten flowers and make way for lush fruit! Ever eaten something that didn't digest well? That probably happened because what you ate combined with the wrong things in your system and became spoiled. When spoiled food is in your system, your breath stinks, you get gas, and, well, you know the rest of the story! You don't eat foods that don't respond well to your system deliberately, and likewise, rotten flowers are simply a knee-jerk reaction to bad experiences that you've unconsciously allowed to take root in your heart. Let the gentle touch of the Master pluck them out and prune you to make room for the delicious fruit He wants to come from your experience. Plants look pretty pathetic when they've been pruned, but wow! When the new growth bursts forth, it is something beautiful to behold.

You're also going to need some fertilizer. The best fertilizer I can think of is prayer. Begin to pray for your future husband every day. Sow prayers for your relationship, for your family, for the call of God to be made clear in both of your lives. Even more importantly, pray that God leads that man to find you. Pray for his eyes to be opened to recognize you as his missing rib. Pray that you will be equipped to meet his needs and he yours. Pray that both of you will have a heart to receive from one another. By doing this you're putting faith into action. Gardeners don't expect the flower to grow immediately after planting the seed. They wait a season. But all the while they're watering, weeding, and fertilizing the ground to keep it healthy in preparation for the birth of a beautiful flower.

Sometimes, you might plant a seed in one spot, but the flower surfaces in another location. The root may travel. So, as you sow, don't look for the blessing to come from the exact spot where you've sown. God might have had you sow in that area to prepare you and to help you practice for what He's going to bring you from another source. Every good gardener knows how to let nature take its course. He knows another secret too: One seed will produce more than one flower or piece of fruit. It will produce a bounty of beauty and goodness to enjoy. So sow prayerfully and expect to reap a rich harvest!

Prayer

Dear Lord, help me to be faithful to Your first call for my life, which is to bear fruit. Let the Holy Spirit show me where to plant seed. May He water it and produce a crop in me that is worthy of Your approval. Let it be a rich crop that others partake of and enjoy. Help me to trust You with the seasons of planting and gathering, as I rest in the knowledge that You will bring forth the increase in my life as You purpose it for Your ultimate glory and my fulfillment, In Jesus' Name. Amen.

Principle #14

Learn How to Dance

When I was in high school I loved to go to dances, but I dreaded the moment the music switched to a slow dance. I always felt like such a klutz when it came to slow dancing. No one had ever officially taught me how to slow dance, so the steps were foreign to me. Everyone else, on the other hand, looked so professional swooping, dipping, and gliding across the floor! It looked so effortless—that is, until I attempted to swoop and glide. I would stiffen up like a board and step on the poor guy's toes. Oh, boy, it was downright embarrassing! My dance partner would always say, "Ease up, baby, just follow me." That was easier said than done. Because I had no idea what he was going to do, I would tense up, making me hesitate a beat after he took a step. By the time I followed we would be completely off the rhythm. To be perfectly honest, I still hadn't gotten it right the last time I attempted!

But when I danced alone, now *that* was a different story! After all, *I* was in control. I remember taking a jazz dance class a few years ago. As we were doing a series of moves across the floor, the dance instructor yelled out, "Michelle, you're not counting!" To which I replied, "Shoot, black people don't count when they're dancing, they just feel the music!" The entire class exploded in laughter. However, I was quite serious! I just had a sense of timing with the music. Inside, I could feel where that next step was supposed to be. So while everyone else around me counted, "And one-two-three, and one-two-three, and one…," I didn't miss a beat. I was right in step because the music and I were one.

And so it is with this thing called submission. Most of us do very well dancing to life's tune when we're on our own. But when it's time to follow a partner, we stumble. We get out of step. We tread on toes. We sometimes just miss it altogether! Why? Perhaps because most of the time we're dancing with a stranger. We're not familiar with our dance partner's rhythm, and we haven't yet learned to anticipate where he might lead us next. We have nothing to base our trust on, and we freeze instead of flow with our partner.

Check Him Out Before the Dance

I believe one of the biggest problems people have with the concept of submission is a lack of trust—a lack of faith, a lack of certainty that if we stay in order, the person we're dancing with will too. I mean, really! How could God tell us to "submit to one another out of reverence for Christ" (Ephesians 5:21) when people are so crazy? Didn't he know people were subject to do as they pleased at our expense? That's why the dating process is so crucial for processing information. Now is the time to find out if this man—who you're thinking you might want to spend the rest of your days with—is submitted to Christ in regard to not only you but *every* aspect of his life. How he spends money. How he interacts with others, both casually and professionally. How he yields to the law and to authorities. How he views what submission *really* means. Better check this out well before the organ starts playing, my friend!

I don't want to go over the same old stuff about submission that you ought to know by now. Since we're discussing a dance, I'd simply like to share a few hors d'oeuvres, food for thought to munch on. I'm sure you know and understand that submission does not mean being a doormat. Submission does mean cooperating with your man, fitting in with your husband's plans, yielding to him as the spiritual head and leader of your family. Submission for him means putting aside his own interests in order to care for you. If both partners have a strong relationship with Christ, this will set the foundational rhythm for a graceful dance. If not, blisters develop from constantly stepping on each other's toes. If this man is fulfilling his God-ordained position in your life, your submission will be a natural response to the love he is pouring out on you. In turn, he will yield more to you because you're not giving him a hard time. Get the picture? There is a complete movement to this waltz!

Submission is not only the plan that keeps down the number of cooks in the kitchen or the number of chiefs in the tribe. It keeps order where there's usually chaos. And above all, it provides protection. Remember what makes the devil flee? That's right, submitting to God, not throwing your weight around. The same applies in a relationship. It's pretty hard for someone to argue with themself. Stubbornness never wins battles; it only paralyzes the army.

Submission—or subjection, placing one's self under the other—means you are able to stand under the principles of the other. Notice the operative word here is *stand*—willingly stand, not sit or lay. It is a stance of your choosing because you see the wisdom of the decision. And even if you can't see clearly at first, you trust that your mate is allowing God to lead you both toward the best solution for the immediate situation. So you continue prayerfully together. God honors your cooperation in this case, like an umbrella covering both of you. Look at it in terms of the simple etiquette of a man walking on the outside as you proceed down the sidewalk together. If a car passes and splashes up water, it gets on him. You've been shielded by his presence. This is God's design throughout the life of your marriage. You may consider yourself to be under, but that man is your covering. If you remove yourself from his protection, you are on your own spiritually and physically. Think about it!

You won't have the same excuse for being out of step that I had in those days of high school dances. Your husband will be a partner you know. Therefore, you'll be moving in each other's rhythms, anticipating each other's dips, mirroring each other's steps. You'll be hotter than Fred Astaire and Ginger Rogers! I mean, in tune!

Master the Steps

Want to know how good a dancer you'll be in marriage? Take a look at how well you dance to your boss's tune, or to the beat of those in authority. Do you follow traffic signs or scoot through when you can? Do you do-si-do well in groups you belong to, or are you always the contrary one who resists conformity? Most importantly, how submitted are you to God? Do you dance to His tune, or do you try to convince Him that you know a better song, a cuter step? I suggest you learn to dance now before you attend the main function in your high heels and hurt yourself or, even worse, you hurt the one you've been waiting for all this time.

Trust me, no man likes to waltz with a bad dancer! If he sees a future of sore toes ahead of him, he'll go in search of a smoother partner. After all, everyone has a difficult time in life. The world is a harsh place. No one wants to come home to someone who is always going in the opposite direction and challenging his every move. Remember, he's looking for a partner who will make him look good, even when he's finding it a little difficult to master a step.

I learned a simple principle when riding the bus one day. If you stand with your knees locked, you'll be thrown off-balance if the bus comes to a sudden halt. But if you stand relaxed with your knees loose, a sudden stop will only make you sway. The same principle applies to life and dancing. The more relaxed and open you are to a change of direction, the less jarring the experience will be. So loosen up and get those dancing shoes ready, girl! Learn how to get into your partner's rhythm and anticipate being able to sing and cut a step, even in the rain!

Prayer

Dear Lord, help me to not insist on my way but to always follow Your lead. Help me to see You in others as You use them to guide me along the way that I should take. Show me the areas where I still battle with being in control. Help me to relax and leave everything concerning me in Your care. I know that the hearts of kings are in Your hands and that You turn them whithersoever You wish. Remind me that You are always on the throne even when I feel my life subjected to the whims of others. Keep me resting in the knowledge that You will never leave me or forsake me, and that it is always safe to follow Your lead, in Jesus' Name. Amen.

Principle #15

Know Who Loves Ya, Baby!

*I*t's important to have a clearly defined understanding of this principle before you put it into practice. If this sounds like a little bit of rehashing, so be it. This seems to be the hardest principle to get across, so forgive me for beating a dead horse if you've got it by now! Why did mama repeatedly tell you *never* to make the first move toward a man? Why do you need to let him call you and do most of the work to get the relationship going? All together now, in unison...I can't hear you! *For your emotional well-being, girlfriend!*

If you want to tell me again what year it is, my answer to you is that now, more than ever, this advice needs to be followed! The bottom line is this: if a man doesn't make the first move toward you—even if you *do* manage to capture his attention for awhile—he will inevitably go off in pursuit of someone who catches his eye and gives him a good challenge. In short, you become temporary filler because he had nothing better to do at the time. Think back on your relationships. Size up the ones where you did the coaxing and nourishing versus the ones where that guy just wouldn't give up until he got your attention. Who got rid of who in each instance? 'Nuff said!

Remember that God doesn't believe in wasting your time. It's time you realized how valuable you are! Why get involved in a relationship if it isn't eventually going to go where you want it to go? Now, it *is* fine for you to have male friends, but if you've set your sights on a man with romance in mind, don't put yourself in a position to be disappointed. Men seem to be able to separate themselves from their emotions much easier than women can. Therefore, he might be all for having fun with you until something better comes along. If that's not something you can handle, don't put yourself out there!

Women love to make up excuses for men like, "Well, maybe he's just shy," or, "What if he lost my number?" Honey, you ought to know by now that when a man wants something, he wants it! And he'll do whatever it takes to get it. Just think back to every guy you didn't want to be bothered with. You ignored him. You didn't send him any cards. You didn't buy him gifts. You never returned his calls, and when he called you, you cut the conversation short. You didn't have time to go out with him every time he asked. What happened? You couldn't get rid of the guy, could you? He just kept calling and calling and calling! I've had men in my life I was downright not friendly to. I know those men had taken lessons from a Timex watch because they took a licking and kept on ticking. Okay, do I have a witness? Mmm hmm, I thought so!

Why couldn't you get rid of those guys? Because you were *a challenge*. And a challenge is a tantalizing thing, even to the most liberated man. Therefore, if you're in a room full of people and your eyeballs land on some guy who you think is awfully cute, you need to keep that comment to yourself and keep right on stepping if he doesn't approach you. Why? Because if he doesn't approach you, he wasn't moved enough by what he saw when he looked at you. "Well, maybe he didn't notice me," you say. Well, if he didn't notice you, all the more reason to leave him where you found him! If you have to make him notice you, you're starting off on the wrong foot already. You're already hotter for him than he is for you, which means you're going to do a lot of things you shouldn't do to get this relationship underway. In your brain, you've sped past Friendship City and set your cruise control for the capital city of Commitment in the State of Marriage. You're already way ahead of yourself! For those who would like to venture that some men are just not the aggressive type, I would be led to conclude that if they dont have a hunter instinct when it comes to pursuing a woman who has caught their eye, they probably are passive in other areas of their lives, such as the job arena, as well.

Two Scenarios

Let's mock up two scenarios on how this little drama could play out. In the first skit you follow your heart's reaction. You either position yourself in such a way that this man eventually is forced to speak to you, or you do that bold, liberated thing and just float right on over to him, introduce yourself, and make small talk. He gets the hint that you're interested, he's flattered, and he responds. He finds out that you are a pretty nice person, so he even goes a step further and takes down your phone number—whether he really wants it or not.

Now your hopes are raised to expect a phone call from him. Maybe he calls and maybe he doesn't. If he calls, you're really on a roll now! You tell your friends everything you know about him. After all, he did call so he's definitely interested, isn't he? This is progress! If he doesn't call, you're disappointed and probably somewhat hurt. You wonder what happened. If you know someone connected to him, you might even ask that person about him and think up an elaborate plan for getting in touch with him.

Let's stretch this drama out a bit and say you two get in touch, whether by your scheming or his calling. You go out. You have a nice time. You're even beginning to develop a relationship when all of a sudden he shifts direction and moves on in pursuit of someone else. You're left feeling very hurt and confused. What happened? You thought everything was going so well. It was. The two of you simply had different agendas. You were interested in having a long-term relationship with him. He just wanted to have a good time. He was unattached, so what's the problem? The problem is that not only has your heart been hurt, so has your pride. You put a lot of work into making this relationship happen, and now your only reward is rejection.

Now let's look at scenario number two. You see a guy and think he's cute. You file that data in the back of your head and resist the urge to stare at him. You continue to mix and mingle. The good-looking guy never approaches you. The evening ends and you go your separate ways. You mention to a girlfriend that you saw the cu-u-test guy at a function the night before, then you move on to another topic. In time you forget about him. He becomes a mere cute face in your personal "cute man file," along with Brad Pitt and Denzel Washington. The difference in this scenario is that now he's simply a passing fancy. He doesn't hurt you, and you have one less wound to nurse. Your heart is still healthy and ready for the man God has ordained to approach you.

Know Who Wants Who

When he sets his sights on you and makes it his business to pursue you and get your attention, honey, you will know that a "Wanted" poster with your picture on it hangs in his heart! Like I said, when a man wants something, he wants what he wants. And he won't take no for an answer! The only thing that can distract a determined man from being hot on the trail of the woman he wants is business. Otherwise, he will be on your case like white on rice. And that's cool, 'cause then you'll be very clear on who wants who.

There was no doubt in anyone's mind who wanted who in the Jacob and Rachel romance. When Jacob laid eyes on her, his whole universe went *bam!* He jumped into action in order to grab her attention. He rolled away the stone of the well, watered her sheep, kissed her, and lifted up his voice and wept! When was the last time a man lifted up his voice and wept after he kissed you? I'm still thinking about that one. How about you?

Genesis chapter twenty-nine goes on to tell us that Jacob loved Rachel and told her father he would work seven years for her hand. When was the last time a man worked to earn you? Here is Jacob working *seven years* for the love of a woman! I mean, he loved him some Rachel! So much so that the Bible says the seven years seemed like a few days to him. Can you imagine? He didn't even get to consummate his love for her until he had worked the full seven years. Then, to top it off, he got tricked into marrying Rachel's sister, Leah, after all that time and had to work *another* seven years for Rachel, which he did willingly! I guess some of us need to take a lesson!

Now, I'm not advocating playing games here. What I'm saying is this: the only way to always be treated by your husband as a valuable commodity is to make sure that he understands *from the beginning* that you are accessible but costly. Set your standards for the future now. For instance, no man should feel comfortable calling you at the last minute inviting you to do something as an afterthought. The man you're interested in should never get the impression that you've been sitting by the phone praying for his call. This is not good, ladies! He should know that he needs to plan ahead when it comes to seeing you because your life is full and your time is valuable. If a special opportunity to do something really wonderful comes up at the last minute and it couldn't be helped, your "yes" should be interpreted as your ability to be incredibly spontaneous, not desperate. Got it?

Keeping yourself busy does two things. It keeps him aware that he is getting a real prize in you (and this *is* scriptural), and it makes you secure because you know that he thinks you're the best thing since sliced bread. The power that comes with being desired is an awesome thing to behold. I personally think it is the best beauty secret in the world. It puts a sparkle in your eyes, adds brilliance to your smile, puts music in your laughter, and makes your countenance glow. All of these add up to a more beautiful, desirable you, which makes him come on stronger, which makes you blossom more and more, which makes him do cartwheels, which...you see the cycle? It's a much better cycle than the cycle of you reaching, him dodging, you cutting him off at the pass, him doing a side-step...you know what I'm talking about!

Set Your Own Pace

"Why does it seem that the woman always has to set the standard for everything?" you may ask. The reality of life is, whether it is in the area of emotional or sexual etiquette, a man will always try a woman. But that's where your power as a woman comes in. Instead of complaining about something that probably won't change anytime soon, use your power! Set the pace and pick the flavor. It's totally up to you how the relationship will go! God can't make him treat you special if you act cheap. If you start off allowing him to be disrespectful of your time, inconsiderate of your feelings, selfish and altogether trifling, don't get upset if he doesn't change after you are committed to him. After all, you gave him your stamp of approval by proceeding with the relationship even after he revealed he was worthless. If you, on the other hand, have politely and in your most ladylike way told that man, "Listem, this is not the type of treatment I am used to or find acceptable; therefore, I think you are not ready for a friendship or relationship with me." One of two things will happen: He will either accept that information as true even though it hurts his ego, or he will reapproach you from a new angle. Just keep in mind, he has already displayed his true colors. Think about it! When you stand before God that "It was the mate you gave me" argument won't work. It didn't work with Adam in the garden after the fall, and it won't work with you. God will simply say, "Yeah, I know about him, but what did I tell you to do?" Two wrongs never have made a right. So stay in your right position. To be perfectly honest, you are the only person you can control.

So stop trying to make things happen. By doing that, you're short-circuiting your own happiness. Stop force-fitting yourself into situations that God wants to shield you from. When you get out from under His umbrella of protection guess what? You get rained on. And that's not His fault, it's yours. So stay put and allow Him to shield you and your heart from unnecessary grief. God knows where you are and where your man is. Pray and ask Him to order your steps so that you meet at His ordained time. Until then, leave every cute man right where you found him unless he approaches you. And when he does approach you, check his references with the Holy Spirit to see if you should give him the time of day or your phone number before you get excited. 'Cause after all, a *Principles* woman knows that if a husband is what she wants, she needs to keep the way clear for his entrance.

Prayer

Dear Heavenly Father, help me to remain in Your lap, wrapped in Your arms as I wait for the appointed day of my mate's arrival. Grant me the gift of keen discernment to see what I need to see. Open my ears to hear what I need to hear as I encounter the men life sends my way. Keep me ever aware of Your presence and Your plan for love in my life. Help me to settle for nothing less than Your perfect design of love for me. Slow the urgent beating of my heart that I might hear and heed the Holy Spirit's instruction. Let me be first and foremost a Principles woman who will be a credit to Your kingdom. Help me to conduct myself as a woman of God at all times, even in the face of temptation. And above all, Lord, I ask that You select the man who is best for me and send him speedily, in Jesus' Name. Amen.

Principle #16

Know What You Want

Now it's time for the big question: Do you want a husband, or do you want to be a wife? Think about that for a minute. There *is* a difference in case you hadn't noticed. If you merely want a husband, you can have a husband. Today! Right now! So obviously we don't just want a *husband*, because otherwise we would all have been married by now. We turned some guys down because we didn't find what we were looking for in them. But how about taking a look at what *he* is looking for? And while we're at it, let's talk about what God is looking for in you as a wife. Have you ever thought about that? Yeah, I know!

Read the Job Description

Would you fill out an application for a job if you didn't know what the job really entailed? And if you don't have a job description, how do you know you want the job? Perhaps you would remove yourself from consideration if you knew the real deal on what was expected of you! And the truth of the matter is, God expects a lot. He wants His mighty men of valor to be well taken care of, and he knows that we women have the power to inspire a man to greatness or reduce him to groveling in the dust. After all, He made us! He doesn't expect us to be perfect, but to be the type of woman and wife that inspires God to write a chapter about us— a la the virtuous woman found in Proverbs 31—we've got to have our act together.

Many singles—Christian or otherwise—who have been waiting some time for a mate get so focused on what they want that they forget the purpose of it! Now, this is *not* a good idea when it comes to marriage. As my friend P.B. Wilson and her husband, Frank, say so appropriately in their book, *The Master's Degree,* we study for every other job on the planet except the most important one of all—the job of making a marriage work.

Now why is that? You'll spend more time being a wife than you will being an employee. Even when you're at work, you are still a wife. The responsibilities of marriage don't end when you walk out of your front door in the morning to go to the office. They go right along with you. You can't retire from marriage after a specific number of years. No, this is a lifelong, life-consuming profession! That is, if you really understand what you are getting yourself into and really take your marriage seriously.

So I submit for your perusal the stats on what a wife really is. And before you continue on with this chapter, I think you should pray first. Some of what I will share with you is so opposite of the world's programming and what you and your girlfriends (you know, the ones who are still single too) have decided that it might take you more than a minute to get in the flow and receive this word. So take a deep breath and ask God to give you an open heart to see and receive this message from His perspective. Also, every time you feel the urge to rebel against the information you're acquiring, mutter this over and over to yourself: "Every good job comes with good benefits and perks" (we'll talk about this later). For now, let's get an understanding of what The Boss upstairs wants from *you!*

Find Your Perfect Fit

First of all, if you are coveting the position of a wife, understand and know that you were made for a man. Mmm, hmm, let me repeat that. You were made, fashioned, and designed to help a man. You were created to be a *help* who would *meet* a specific man's specific needs. Someone asked me the other day if I thought there was only one mate for each person. My reply to them—and to you—is this: When God decided that Adam needed a partner, He did not create Mary, Sue, and Jill and then tell Adam to take his pick. He created Eve from Adam's rib. She actually was a *part* of Adam. She didn't just happen by; she was deliberately crafted to fit him. Get the idea? So yes, it is highly likely that there's several men out there who you could get along with and have a decent relationship with. However, I believe that God knows who would be the best match for you. He designed you to "fit" someone's rib cage.

Now about that rib cage—why was woman taken from the rib of man? Well, the rib cage covers the body's vital organs. Are you getting the picture of how important you are? You have the capacity to affect everything vital in your mate's life. This is no small thing! So don't let people in the world convince you that the role of a woman is a powerless thing. No statement is more incorrect than that one. In fact, I believe that statement is a major tactic the enemy uses to move us away from God and send us in pursuit of our own interests.

Anyway, you were made, fashioned, and designed to be a "help-meet" to your man. Man was not made for you, you were made for man. Now don't get all excited! We'll take a look at the man's role when we're finished dealing with ourselves. A guy's requirements are no walk in the park, either. After all, God is fair. Anyhow, moving on! Man needed help, and women got drafted for the job. We should consider this an honor. Men do not function well without us. (God said it, not me!) I remind Him all the time that He said, "It is not good for the man to be alone" (Genesis 2:18 NIV). And then I gently suggest that, because I'm still sitting here, my husband is out there wandering around alone too (or at least, I hope so!). And God should do something about it as soon as possible because I'm sure that guy could use my help.

Be a Life-Bearer

I did a study of every biblical encounter of a man discovering his mate and found something quite interesting. In every case, the women were doing something nurturing. Rebekah's husband found her at a well, and so did Rachel's. Esther had been purified and soaked in oil for twelve months, Ruth was gathering grain, Abigail came bearing food, and even Bathsheba was bathing herself. The Shulamite woman was working in a vineyard. See what I mean? I don't believe this is an accident! Women are life-bearers. The name Eve means "to give life." Men need nurturing and nourishing. They don't take very good care of themselves, and they're basically clueless in a lot of areas that come as second nature to us. We were created this way in order to be interdependent. God never meant for men and women to operate as separate islands, drifting aimlessly through life.

I recently met a woman who'd allowed her husband to just slip through her fingers. As she began to relate her story to me, the root of her problem became very clear. She told me a long-winded tale about how, ever since she had been married to this man, he had moved here, there, and everywhere. He was never able to settle in one place. When they first got married he wanted to move to a different city, but she wanted to stay close to her mother. She refused to go with him, so he went ahead of her to establish his career and a home for them. After some time she joined him, but soon moved back close to her mother. He tried returning to her city but his career fizzled there, so he moved to a new city and once again established a home for her. She joined him for a time, then returned to mother. She repeated this cycle several times until he eventually grew weary, contemplated a divorce, and moved to London. When I met her she was wondering if she should join him in London to try to work things out.

As I listened in complete fascination she said, "I still love him. He's a good man; I just want him to get his act together." To which I replied: "Honey, he can't because you won't help! What is this nonsense? Did you marry him or your mother? What happened to the idea of 'leaving and cleaving' here? You are out of spiritual order! You should thank God this man still wants to be bothered with you. Pack your bags and go to London! Do not pass go. Do not collect $200. Go and fix your marriage by being obedient to God." She looked at me as if I'd given her some new revelation and agreed to do as I had advised. I, on the other hand, walked away completely befuddled over the whole conversation.

In Genesis chapter twenty-four Abraham sends his servant to find a wife for his son Isaac. His instructions are very clear. The servant is instructed to go to Abraham's homeland, to his relatives, and find a wife for Isaac. The servant then asks what will happen if he can't find a woman who will travel so far away from home. Will he, then, take Isaac to live there? Abraham says no, if she is unwilling to come back with him, forget it. Under no circumstances was Isaac supposed to pack up and move to where this woman was. That would put him out of his proper position, which would affect his inheritance.

When the servant arrived in Abraham's homeland, he prayed and asked God to help him recognize the right woman based on her willingness to serve him as well as his camels. Why was this important? Because a *Principles* woman understands the importance of looking out for the well-being of everything that concerns her husband. In Rebekah's day it was important to recognize the role livestock played in the wealth of its owner. Well, along came Rebekah, who offered the servant water and immediately set about watering the camels as well. This was a signal to the servant that here was a wise as well as beautiful woman. Rebekah was smart and understood her position. Her family was in no hurry to be separated from her, but she agreed to leave them and go with the servant.

You must be willing to leave and cleave. You are not marrying a family (although life will definitely be more peaceful if you get along with your in-laws!); you are married to *one person*. Rebekah's story ends by noting that Rebekah was a special comfort to Isaac. So not only was she beautiful, willing to serve, strong enough to physically tend to necessary chores, mindful of caring for her husband's possessions, but she was also a special comfort. A *Principles* woman if there ever was one!

Cover Him in Prayer

In the book of Esther we find Queen Esther informing her husband of a plot against his life. A *Principles* wife watches her husband's back. She uncovers the work of the enemy in his life and covers him in prayer. Another *Principles* woman, Abigail, interme-diated a situation that could have cost her husband his life. A good wife knows how to quietly diffuse the mistakes of her husband without making it painful and embarrassing for him. She ministers peace, focus, and sound reasoning to her husband. She keeps him ever-mindful of the call of God upon his life, especially in the face of his struggles.

Give Him Praise and Wealth

The Shulamite woman praised her husband. Ladies, a little praise goes a long way with a man! A little praise inspires him to try a little harder, dig a little deeper, do a little better. Talk about the power of life and death being in the tongue! In one short sen-tence, you can inspire a man to greatness or cause him to believe he is a no-good failure. Not only did the Shulamite woman praise her man, she added to his wealth. When she married King Solomon she gladly gave her vineyard and profits to him. Ready to merge those bank accounts, ladies? How about those last names? The Bible does not say "and the two shall become hyphenated," it says that the two shall become *one*. That man might go along with you keeping your last name, but inside he might quietly resent it. This, then, will become an open door for the enemy to cause con-fusion and strife in the unity of your home. But this is a separate and very deep topic that has important spiritual ramifications. Settle your identity issues before you get married, please. It is *not* worth the chaos it can create!

Let's revisit the Proverbs 31 woman for a minute. She, too, added to her husband's wealth with her enterprising spirit. Verse 16 says, "She considers a [new] field before she buys or accepts it [expanding prudently and not courting neglect of her present duties by assuming other duties]; with her savings [of time and strength] she plants fruitful vines in her vineyard" (Proverbs 31:16, AMP). But that is just the beginning of her attributes! This one statement about her covers them all: "Her husband can trust her, and she will greatly enrich his life. She will not hinder him but help him all her life" (Proverbs 31:11-12 NLT). The Amplified Version reads, "The heart of her husband trusts in her confidently and relies on and believes in her securely, so that he has no lack of [honest] gain or need of [dishonest] spoil. She comforts, encourages, and does him only good as long as there is life within her." I believe this passage explains itself.

Give Him a Good Rep.

And last, but certainly not least, a wife is also responsible for her husband's good reputation. I can never stress this enough! You can affect a man's work and his ministry. One of the qualifications for a bishop or a deacon in the book of First Timothy is that his household must be in order. When a man is being considered for partnership in a firm, the wife is scrutinized. Many are leary of unmarried men holding political office or being promoted to higher levels of corporate management. Why? Because the presence of a good woman in a man's life somehow validates him as a responsible, grounded individual. When his home life is stable, a man will be focused and able to excel in everything he does. When his home is out of order, it can lead to inefficiency in the marketplace and bouts of immorality. You have the key to your man's greatness in your hands, so be careful how you use it.

Every woman who has failed in this area has found herself displaced either physically or emotionally. Queen Vashti forfeited her position when she refused to come when the king called her. She was seen as a threat to the balance of the entire kingdom, and the princes reasoned that their wives would soon follow Queen Vashti in this sort of disobedience and lack of respect. Michal despised David's celebratory dance before the Lord and remained unfruitful (childless) for the rest of her days. I believe it's safe to say she also forfeited David's love that day as well. The word unfruitful has serious connotations to it. It suggests her entire life became empty and barren after attempting to quench her husband's spirit. What an awful existence—loveless and fruitless. Jezebel lost out because she wouldn't allow her husband to be a man. Her actions cost both of them their lives. Every time a woman emasculates a man, it kills something inside of them both.

Keep Him in Order

A good wife keeps everything concerning her husband in order—his home, his children, herself. If she doesn't, everything in his world suffers—his job, his self-esteem, his marital relationship. All of it will systematically fall into a state of disarray. Are you beginning to see the power you have to make or break a man? To bless or curse his existence? To fill his world with light or darkness? To wreck his reputation or set him up to be respected? It's all on you! When a man runs for political office, what is the first thing they check out? You got it—his wife! People make judgments about him based on the character of his wife and his relationship with her. Think about it!

First Corinthians 11:7 says that the woman is the glory of the man. Remember how, when the ark of the Lord was taken from Israel, the people lapsed into despair because the "glory of the Lord" had departed from Israel? To "be the glory of" is to derive significance from. Israel was feared because the glory of the Lord was in its midst. The ark validated the Israelites as a force to be reckoned with. They had heavy-duty backing. They walked in confidence because they knew their alliance with God covered them. They also knew that when the glory departed, they were open targets— sitting ducks, so to speak—for the enemy to assault at will. Alone, they would have no defense against the strength of the enemy. Are you getting an idea of how important this wife thing is?

Know Your Role

Once married, your primary identity must be that of being your husband's wife and the mother of your children. Then you are free to claim your secondary identity as businesswoman extraordinaire, or minister, or whatever else you dream of doing. I know this flies in the face of modern-day philosophy, but get a grip! A place of honor and high esteem, the role of a wife and mother is no shabby position. It is hard work that requires true genius in order to perform with excellence. You are the power base and the glory of your home. Without you, the inhabitants of that home fall apart. When homes fall apart, neighborhoods are affected; when neighborhoods are in disarray, it desroys the community. The community affects the city. The city, the state. The state, the nation. The nation, the world.... Whew! It's a chain reaction, and it can all begin at your house. One cancer cell can grow, consume an entire body and rob a whole family of one precious life. Every one is affected by one small germ. Are you hearing me? Selah— pause and ponder this—as they say in the psalms. You were created for the man, he was not created for you. If you find you differ with me here, read 1 Corinthians 7-12 and talk to God about it. This passage is about understanding the value of your position through the eyes of God. And it's about the long-term rewards you reap when you "Stand By Your Man." As the popular adage declares, "Behind every good man there's a good woman." No one ever thinks he stands alone!

Proverbs 31 gives us a rather long list of a *Principles* wife's virtues. A *Principles* wife is trustworthy, industrious, hardworking, energetic, frugal, wise, compassionate, resourceful, dignified, kind, thinks ahead, anticipates needs, and fears the Lord. And the key attribute out of the entire chapter is this: "She will greatly enrich his life. She will not hinder him, but will help him all her life." Are you ready for this? Is this what you have in mind as you consider marriage for yourself? "For which of you, intending to build a tower, sitteth not down first, and counteth the cost, whether he have sufficient to finish it?" (Luke 14:28 KJV).

What Are You Bringing to the Party?

As a young girl in grammar school, I was sitting in class enjoying a flavorful piece of gum when my teacher walked up to me and said, "Well, young lady, did you bring enough gum for the rest of the class?" Of course I hadn't! I'd only had myself in mind when I stopped at the store on my way to school. And so it is with those of us who are marriage-minded. On the way to matrimony many of us only have ourselves in mind. How this state of being will make *me* happy. Complete *me*. Provide *me* with the stability, love, and validation I've been looking for. Give *me* the child I've been wanting to have. But what are *you* bringing to the party? What do you have to *offer*? What are you planning to *give*? Are you coming with a couple of marbles to exchange? Are you willing to bring a casserole and leave the plate?

I recall a scene from the movie *The Wiz*, an adaptation of *The Wizard of Oz*, that left a lasting impression in my mind. In this scene Dorothy, Scarecrow, Tin Man, and the Cowardly Lion finally encounter the wizard, whose grand reputation has preceded him. Their dismay and disappointment at finding an ordinary, average person, who had his own fears and needs, was overwhelming. This was not what they had bargained for at all! They were in search of some amazing person who could magically perfect their lives. And here was this little, insignificant man telling them to discover what they were looking for within themselves.

Like the characters in *The Wiz*, some of us will be very disappointed with marriage if our expectations are all wrong. Some of us are still tripping down the yellow brick road, searching for the wizard to fill our hearts and help us find our way home. But that ain't hap'nin'. If you're only focused on what you'll get without considering what you'll have to give, you are in trouble. But I'm confident that won't happen to anyone reading this, because *Principles* women know that love is all about giving and giving and giving again!

So! You want to be married, do you? Do you want a husband or do you want to be a wife? That is the question! Your answer should be that you want both. Now you're ready.

Prayer

Dear Heavenly Father, continue to prepare me to be a blessing to the man You've created me to help. Deposit in me everything I need to pour into his life. Help me to be an oasis for him, a place of refreshment. Help me to equip him to serve and glorify You in every area of his life. Give me Your love and care for him. Help me to serve him and be a gift to him all his days. Help me to be not only his wife, but his friend, companion, and lover. Help me to be all that You've ordained me to be for him, in Jesus' Name. Amen.

Know If He's the One

*D*on't think I've let the men escape in this book. Now that you know what you're supposed to be doing, you need to know what *he's* supposed to be doing too. After all, how will you know if *he's* the one? It's not enough to think you heard a voice saying, "This is the one!" Many women have been deceived this way. They have married men they would never have looked at otherwise, and then turned around and blamed a horrible marriage on God. I'm sorry, but I have a huge problem with that. God never moves contrary to His Word. He will never lead you to marry someone who is not good husband material.

Some women have reasoned that God wanted to teach them some great deep lesson, and the only way He could do this was by having them marry men who literally ran them through the mill. That doesn't sound like the God I know. The only story in the Bible that sounded anything like this is the story of Hosea and Gomer which is found in the book of Hosea. God had Hosea marry a loose, immoral woman in order to make a prophetic statement to the Israelites about their attitude toward Him and to illustrate a call to repentance and restoration. I do not believe that God calls His prophets today to do illustrative prophecies. Instead, He sends His Word through them to rebuke, correct, and edify. Therefore, if He wants to teach you a lesson, He doesn't need to use a marriage that doesn't glorify Him to do it. This is not conducive to Kingdom business, but we'll talk more about that later!

Finding Good Husband Material

So how do you know if the man before you is husband material? Let's take a look at what the Word of God says. That works better then coming up with something that just sounds good off the top of our heads. Let's revisit the wells. You remember how Rebekah was willing to leave her family and her familiar surroundings to go to her husband? Well, it's important to note that a man must be willing to do the same.

I find it significant that Abraham decided it was time for Isaac to be married after his mother died. We all know about that special bond between a mother and her son. Unfortunately, some mothers do not raise their sons to be good husbands, and this is detrimental in the long run. It can be the ruin of many a good man. By the time this man shows up on your doorstep, he has acquired a bunch of bad habits and even stranger expectations of a wife's role, based on his experiences with his mother. Even worse, many a mother has continued to manipulate her son throughout his marriage. This causes countless sincere wives unnecessary grief. A man must be willing to cut the cord between himself and mama. He must be willing to "leave and cleave." Otherwise, if he isn't, you will have big problems!

The Bible says something else on this topic that I find significant. It says that Isaac brought Rebekah into his mother's tent, she became his wife, he loved her very much, and she was a special comfort to him after the death of his mother. This happens in the very last verse of the twenty-fourth chapter. In essence, Rebekah became the extension of Isaac's experience with a woman. An evolution took place. Rebekah in no way could ever replace Isaac's mother, and that was not her or God's intention. But to extend the love relationship to another level—this was divine! It was done in complete spiritual order. Isaac took Rebekah into a place of security and loved her. Her response to his love was to become a special comfort. She gave him the kind of comfort his mother could not give. Yet the mother role is one that she could not fill. Each role is distinct and has its own unique place and merit, but they cannot and should not overlap. A good husband will be clear on where you fit in his life.

Let's move on to the next well. It was after Jacob left mama Rebekah that he spotted Rachel. He needed a clean break from parental ties and, in essence, a release to cleave to his God-ordained spouse. When Jacob got a glimpse of Rachel in the twenty-ninth chapter of Genesis, he immediately sprang into action. He rolled away the stone from the mouth of the well and watered her father's flocks. No one else but Jacob felt a pressing need to do this. Everyone else was waiting until it was convenient for all the flocks. Rachel was not the primary focus in their minds. But she was to Jacob. He immediately exhibited strength and a willingness to serve her and look out for her provision. He rolled the stone away.

I remember once when I was going through a difficult time, a pastor friend asked me, "What is a rock?" I answered, "It's an inanimate object." He rolled his eyes at me and said, "No, girl, keep it simple. A rock is a hard thing." He then went on to tell me I should take all the hard things in my life and build an altar to the Lord with them. So, in that same way, Jacob was there to move the hard things out of Rachel's path—the things that stopped the flow of God, in a sense. He released the rivers of living water to come forth and nourish her flocks. Like Jacob, your husband should be strong in the Lord. He should be concerned about your well-being and your provision in the natural as well as the spiritual. He should be your priest.

Back in biblical days, even though the marriage contract was arranged quite early in a daughter's life, she stayed in her parents' home until her future husband had acquired enough money to provide a home and take care of her properly. In other words, that girl was not permitted to leave and live with her husband until he was able to rightly take care of her. No Mr. Moms existed back then!

Jacob worked seven years to earn Rachel's hand in marriage. The Bible says the seven years he waited were like just a few days to him. And as you know, after that Rachel's father pulled a switch on Jacob and gave him Rachel's sister, Leah, instead. He only agreed to give Rachel to Jacob if he worked *another* seven years. And Jacob agreed to it! Now, that is some serious love! Your husband will want to work for your affection as well as your provision. He will do his best to give you a nice home and a comfortable existence. A real man is not at ease with it being any other way. It will bother him if he cannot provide for you. And it won't be because of pride. It'll be because it's built into his spirit to do so!

When Ruth, another *Principles* woman, made her way to the threshing floor to let Boaz know her need for a kinsman-redeemer, he responded in some very significant ways. First Boaz agreed to do what was necessary to fulfill Ruth's need. He then covered her until the early morning. After that, he filled her bags with grain and sent her home before anyone could see her leaving and think the wrong thing.

I think it's interesting that the word "redeemer" is used in this instance. Read the account for yourself in the third chapter of Ruth. Boaz was stirred to "redeem" Ruth, to save her from her situation of being a widow with no sons, forced to glean the fields for food. He rose to the occasion, presenting the matter to Ruth's next of kin, a man who was perfectly willing to redeem the land that belonged to Ruth's mother-in-law's family *but* was not up for the wife who would come along as part of the package deal. Like so many men today, he wanted to reap the benefits without taking any responsibility! So the next man in line was Boaz, and he followed through. Not only was he willing to redeem Ruth, he was also willing to cover her. He was willing to protect her reputation and help her avoid the appearance of evil. He was willing to make provision for her, feed her, and satisfy her needs. And he felt honored to have her attention!

Ephesians 5:25-28 says, "And you husbands must love your wives with the same love Christ showed the church. He gave up his life for her to make her holy and clean, washed by baptism and God's word. He did this to present her to himself as a glorious church without a spot or wrinkle or any other blemish. Instead, she will be holy and without fault. In the same way, husbands ought to love their wives as they love their own bodies. For a man is actually loving himself when he loves his wife" (NLT). *This* is sacrificial love. This type of love places others' needs above your own and nurtures to the utmost.

Boaz redeemed Ruth. He pledged his protection and provision over her. This same character will be in the heart of the man who God chooses for you. These desires will be instinctual in him. He will be concerned for your welfare and whereabouts at all times. You should never have to ask him where he's been. The man who has a heart for you will always let you know where he can be reached, and he'll always want to know how he can reach you. This isn't out of nosiness and control; it stems from genuine concern. Leaving you behind would be like leaving a piece of himself behind.

Boaz covered and protected Ruth in the dark. How comforting! Can you imagine how safe she must have felt? Your husband should make you feel secure. You should be able to rest in his statement, "I'll take care of it," release the matter, and allow him to follow through. And lastly, Boaz filled Ruth with good things. He didn't send her away empty-handed while she waited for him to work out the situation. The man who God has for you won't leave you guessing. Your heart will be full of the things he has poured into you. You won't have to go asking friends to dissect every little thing he said or did to find the clue to his intentions. His actions, as well as his words, will be very clear. Remember, talk is cheap but following through with action can be very expensive. This is the true acid test!

What Has He Done for You Lately?

Throughout the Bible men demonstrated the heart of God toward women. David killed hundreds of Philistines to gain the hand of Michal. Is your man willing to do exploits for you? For the Shulamite woman, Solomon built an immense home that resembled the surroundings she was used to, except on a grander scale. Is that man striving to keep you in the lifestyle to which you are accustomed or better? He also praised her beauty continually. Is that man fluffing up your ego and romancing you? King Xerxes killed Esther's enemy. Is your man covering you in prayer and putting the enemy to flight in your life? Not only did he do away with her enemies, but he offered Esther up to half of his kingdom. Is the man in your life generous and willing to share all he has with you, or is he looking for a handout? Small wonder Janet Jackson sings, "What Have You Done for Me Lately?" and small wonder so many women identify with that song! They feel unfulfilled. They feel as if something is missing in the way their men treat them. However, here I must admit that the lowered standards of many women desperately in search of a mate have certainly contributed to men not rising to the full status of doing their "man thing." The Bible warns us of the deterioration of women's standards by stating in Isaiah 4:1 that in the last days "seven women shall take hold on one man, saying, 'We will eat our own bread, and wear our own apparel; only let us be called by thy name, to take away our reproach'" (KJV). Another translation says, "so we won't be mocked as old maids." That is not our calling ladies, to settle for scraps to validate our identity as women. We are now part of a royal priesthood in Christ, set apart to live by a higher standard.

It's built into a man's spirit to do exploits for his woman, to lavish her with care and protect her. When he's falling down on the job, it's time to do a Holy Ghost check to find out what's wrong. Either you are not giving him room to be the man he was created to be, or his heart is not in the right place toward you. In either case, someone needs to get with the program or else release the relationship back to God and move on. Do not make up excuses for a man, and do not nag or ask questions. Remember, a man will do exactly what he wants to do. And when he wants something bad enough, he'll do whatever he has to do to get it!

I must take note here to caution those of you who have been on your own for a while. Please! When a man comes into your life who wants to be the man God has called him to be in your life, be willing to release the reins and let him handle the carriage. A lot of men complain that when they try to rise to the occasion of taking the lead, they are met with resistance. After experiencing this repeatedly, they forfeit their role altogether in quiet resentment. You, in turn, lose respect for the poor guy, never realizing your contribution to the problem. So be open to being swept off your feet. He can handle your weight if you let him!

A male friend of mine once told me I'd never get someone to marry me because no man would ever put up with my schedule. My response to his comment was the man who I was fashioned for would either wait until I got back or give me a good reason to stay home. And he had to admit that I had a strong point! I was not in the least bit worried by what he said because I know that I was created from some man's rib. When we encounter one another, he won't be able to help himself because I'm his missing piece. He will be able to accommodate all that I am because I will be the extension of all that he is. Remember that rib cage is a picture of the circumference or circle of a life. The woman is taken from that circle. You are to be a comfortable fit, slipping neatly into place, not causing a pain in his side!

The same will go for you when you encounter your "missing rib cage." Even the things that drive others to distraction about you, he'll be able to take in stride. They are familiar things to his spirit if not his intellect. He will know you because you are a part of him. Now if you say you've never known how a man was supposed to treat you, you no longer have an excuse. It's all right there in your Daddy's book, the Bible. He wants someone who will love you the way He does, and don't you forget it!

Prayer

Heavenly Father, I ask that even now You will pour into my husband all that You want him to be for me. Build him up, fill him with Yourself, and give him a heart that beats for the things that concern You. Order his steps to find me. Help him to be able to receive the help You've created me to give. Fill him with the knowledge of who I am and what I need. Grant him a tender spirit that hears my unspoken cries. Bless the work of his hands and cause him to prosper in all that he does. Keep him unto the day that we meet. Encourage and strengthen his heart to wait on You, to wait for me, in Jesus' Name. Amen.

Principle #18

Master the
Art of Housekeeping

*A*ll right, I really didn't think I had to deal with this topic since I assumed all *Principles* women knew better, but here goes. It's crucial that we master the art of housekeeping. As in keeping our own address. You got it—I'm addressing the subject of living together. Don't, under any circumstances, move in with your friend, significant other, intended—whatever you want to call him. I thought you knew, girlfriend! Finances, premarital test, convenience...none of these excuses hold up with God. Live with your sister, your brother, your best friend, but *puh-leeze!* Do not live with that man! You are setting yourself up for more problems than you will ever need.

Stop making it easy for these men not to make a commitment! You move in and end up cleaning, cooking, doing the laundry, being a wife before it's time (which is the recipe for sour relationships as well as sour wine). I know all about it. I've been there in my B.C. (before Christ) days. If you break this rule, you'll end up breaking several others because the temptation will be too great. It will be easier to fall into premarital sex if you're not there already.

If you are living together and *not* having sex, the tension you are creating will be enough to break up the relationship. If you *are* having sex and trying to still maintain a relationship with God, the guilt you both experience will make you resent one another and will eventually ruin the intimacy you thought you were creating. Even the secular world knows that living together is a shaky proposition if a sound marriage is what you're after. According to research, more marriages fail among the live-in crowd than among those who waited until they were married to share living quarters. Please do not slip and slide across the pond of God's grace and ask Him to bless your mess. Remember, ice is thin and can crack at any time. Do not hold God responsible for the misery you've created for yourself.

And what about how living together affects those outside of your household? You can scream to high heaven that you are abstaining, but the situation leaves too much room for the imagination of onlookers to run rampant. And it makes you a stumbling block for others. Remember, everything you do affects the reputation of your Heavenly Father and the rest of the body of Christ. Why do you think He admonished us to "abstain from all appearance of evil"? (I Thessalonians 5:22 KJV).

David understood this concept well. He said, "He leads me in the paths of righteousness for His name's sake" (Psalm 23:3 NKJV). What is the first thing people say when they see a Christian doing something that they know is ungodly behavior? "I thought she was a Christian!" The world is looking for someone who is really walking the walk and not just talking it. Now is the time for all *Principles* women to rise to the occasion of being the precious vessels they were created to be.

Principles women do not lower their standards and settle for living arrangements that are beneath their station in life. If a man wants to take you home, he should be willing to pay the price. Your mother told you a million times, "Why buy the cow when you can get the milk for free?" I second the motion!

Desperation and impatience twist our thinking and pull us into error and deception every time. Don't fall into this trap! Just as living with a man does not deepen or guarantee his conviction of love for you, neither will having his baby out of wedlock. I realize mistakes happen, but for women who take this as a course of action to solidify their connection to a man, this is the worst move they can make. Even if that man chooses to do "the right thing" by her, namely get married, he will quietly resent her for the duration of their relationship. He will feel that she deliberately trapped him, and what do trapped animals do? They do anything to escape.

The Bible paints a pitiful tale of Leah doggedly trying to win Jacob's love by having baby after baby. Every time she had a baby she said to herself, "Perhaps he will love me now that I've given him a son." But Jacob loved Rachel and that was that. After a while, Leah got a clue and decided to turn her affections toward the Lord. She named her fourth son Judah, which means "Praise." She said, "Now I will praise the Lord" (read Genesis 29:31-35), stopped looking for Jacob's praise, and decided to turn her affections to the Lord instead.

Focus on the One

That is what a lot of us need to do. Stop looking for love in all the wrong places and through all the wrong methods, and focus on the One who has always loved you with an everlasting love. When you fall in love with Jesus, He will pour Himself out to you and love you like you've never been loved before. As you become complete in His love, you'll find yourself more self-satisfied than you've ever been. That is the moment you become an Irresistible Woman, the type of woman that a man has to have. You are not relying on anyone for your happiness. You are a complete woman, in love with her life and her God.

Principles women must remember that we are not of this world, we are called to a higher standard of living. We will not fulfill that calling with below-the-bottom-of-the-barrel expectations. For those of you who are single parents, this chapter is not written to condemn you. God is in the forgiveness business, and, as I said, mistakes do happen. You can be comforted in the knowledge that God promises to be a Father to the fatherless, and you can share this with your child. But now that we've come into the knowledge of Christ and the Word of God, we can avoid costly mistakes by being obedient to His Word.

Think About the Child

If we're not putting ourselves in the direct line of fire for sexual temptation, we stand a better chance of not falling into a situation that can affect not only our own lives forever. It will also affect the father of your child as well as the child that comes into the world and suffers the consequences of having an absentee father. In the Old Testament, illegitimate children could not enter into the congregation of the Lord for ten generations. Thank God the curse of the law is broken through Jesus Christ. Still, in many instances—even though we experience the forgiveness of God— illegitimate children still experience a struggle for identity and self-validation when one of the parents is absent. This struggle is diminished if this child was conceived by mutual choice. God will work with mistakes, but willful actions usually cost us much more than we are ever willing to pay.

Now some of you might want to have a baby simply because you want one. How do you rationalize that train of thought with God? Having a child should be about more than your personal desires. You are not the only one involved here. If you truly have a heart for children, there are plenty of foster children waiting for a loving person to come into their lives and offer them a stable home and existence. There are also children from broken homes who would love to have a positive example and mentor in their lives. This is the true test of your Christianity. The Bible says that pure and undefiled religion before God and the Father is this, "To care for the fatherless and widows in their affliction, and to refuse to let the world corrupt us" (James 1:27). For those who say they have not been "led" to do these things, God does not need to lead you to do what He has already written. God is not in the business of repeating Himself. If He has written it in His word, that is His formal call to action to you.

This new attitude that we no longer have to wait for a husband to have children is nothing more than worldly thinking. This is not God's design. Listening to the world results in deep and lasting consequences for you, the child you bear, and those who inhabit your world. Our flubbubs reach beyond ourselves in every instance. Let's aim for the type of existence God meant for us to have, and follow His directions carefully to avoid life-scarring injuries.

Principles women do not conduct themselves like the women Timothy spoke about in 2 Timothy 3 (KJV) where he states that "silly women laden with sins, led away with divers lusts, ever learning, and never able to come to the knowledge of the truth" would be led away by those who loved pleasure rather than God. Those same women act as if they are religious, but they deny the power that could make them godly. So don't let the clanging of your biological clock drown out the voice of God's sound reason!

Now if you're worried about your biological clock, treat it like an alarm clock early in the morning. Push the snooze button, turn it off, and go find a child to mentor. Find a married couple that needs a break for the weekend and take care of their children. Then come back and tell me about that clock. I bet it won't be ticking so loudly!

Purpose in your heart to be a *Principles* woman. One who keeps her personal and spiritual house clean and sanctified for the man that God wants to present her to. If you're presently living with someone, your house is too crowded. Fix your situation as soon as possible and get on with God's plan for your life. If you are considering living with someone, perish the thought! Your house belongs to God, and all others who enter without His blessing are trespassers. Remember, your house is precious. Keep it well until God releases you to open the door.

Prayer

Dear Heavenly Father, I sanctify my house and set it apart for Your glory alone. Help me to encounter You in every room and bask in the comfort of Your presence. Keep me, cover me, and help me to remain complete in love. Forgive me for any offenses I may have committed against You in thought, word, or action. Cleanse me, refresh me, and renew a right spirit in me that I may walk after Your precepts. Quiet the longings of my flesh and strengthen the call of Your spirit within me, in Jesus' Name. Amen.

The Pleasure Principle

*S*o now that you're clear on what everybody's role should be, are you ready to visit the place of higher learning? Marriage is truly an advanced-level college course in Christianity, and I think everyone should be required to take an entry-level exam. After all, would you stay put on a plane if you found out that the pilot had never attended flight school and was going up in your aircraft just for training? I think you'd suggest that they experimented with someone else's life and luggage, wouldn't you? Yet many of us are experimenting with other people's lives within the institution of marriage.

I find it sad that, in a world which prides itself on being in the know about everything, so little attention is paid to a very important thing that affects all of society—marriage. It seems like no one really knows why they get married. You hear comments like, "Well, I decided it was time to settle down," or "I just knew I wanted to have this person around all the time," or "It seemed like the right thing to do." How lame! What these people are really telling me is that they don't really know why they did it, which usually means that they don't know where they're going as a couple. Kinda reminds me of a song from the seventies that begged the question, "Now that we've found love what are we gonna do with it?" What should your goal be once you're married? If you don't understand the purpose of marriage, you won't have a clue how to answer that question.

The Purpose of Marriage

So why did God come up with this thing called marriage? Paul concluded in Ephesians that two people becoming one was a mystery. No kidding! At any rate, God ordained marriage. The clue as to why He did this is found when we look at why He created man and woman in the first place. God created man to multiply and have dominion over all that He had created on the earth. And He created woman to assist man in his assignment. Everything else in the earth multiplied after its own kind, and we are expected to do the same. As children of God we should multiply—or give birth—to more godly people. We are expected to dominate the works of the enemy by becoming a team that is mighty in the spirit. Solomon wrote in Ecclesiastes 4:12, "If one prevail against him, two shall withstand him; and a threefold cord is not quickly broken" (KJV). The third cord—Christ Himself—keeps the cord from unraveling.

Try this little experiment in order to understand what Solomon was saying. Take two strands of rope or hair and twist them together. Now let go. If the strands didn't unravel on their own, one tug was all it took, right? Now take three strands of rope or hair and braid them. Much more secure, isn't it? I've had my hair braided during the summer and believe me, I always think of this passage when I have to sit and take them all down! It takes forever to get those things undone, and that's the power of the three-fold cord. Perhaps this is why Jesus chose to send the disciples out two by two as well. He knew the value of partnership in warfare. And believe you me, whether you want to acknowledge it or not, we are in a war against the forces of darkness every day. We could use all the assistance we can get!

So if marriage was created to multiply more beings in God's image on the face of the earth, what exactly is His image? We are told in the Bible that God is spirit and those who worship Him must worship Him in spirit and in truth (John 4:24). So we are a spirit, possessing a soul and dwelling in a body. We are a reflection of God the Father, the Son, and the Holy Spirit. This is the complete image of God. Remember, God said, "Let *us* make man in *our* image, after *our* likeness" (Genesis 1:26 KJV, emphasis added). So we can hope that, when we look like Him, we will also have His mannerisms. We can use the authority we've been given to walk in the power of the spirit, destroying the work of the enemy over our family, our cities, and our world. Married or single, that is our assignment. But as we enter the marriage arena, our assignment expands and we move up another tier. So let's move on!

Hebrews 13:4 tells us that marriage is honorable. Honorable to whom? Honorable to God, that's who! Why is marriage to be held in honor as something esteemed, worthy, and precious? Because it is the very reflection of the type of union God intends to have with us. His goal is to be one with us. He wants us to experience the same type of oneness with Him that He experiences with the Holy Spirit and Jesus. They're so tight they are literally referred to as the "Three in One." And so they are. Though they are capable of moving independently of one another, they do not. They walk in constant agreement. Only once in the history of God did a moment of separation exist between them. That moment occurred when Jesus hung on the cross and became sin for us. This is the only time God ever turned His face away and pulled back from His Son because God, as holiness Himself, could not behold sin. Up to this point everything they had ever done, they had done together.

And now we stand as the reflection of their image, being a spirit that possesses a soul that is clothed in a body, created for God's own pleasure. This certainly shatters the pleasure principle as we know it. And here you were thinking you were here on earth to pursue your own pleasure and find ways to delight yourself. Sorry to pull your coat tail, but you had a major string hanging if that was your thinking. My Bible says, "Delight yourself in the LORD, and He will give you the desires of your heart" (Psalm 37:4 NIV). "When a man's [or a woman's] ways please the LORD, He makes even [their] enemies to be at peace with them" (Proverbs 16:7 NKJV). How glorious! The picture comes full circle. I want you to catch this revelation: spirit, soul, body. A reflection of God, the Holy Spirit, and

Jesus Himself. Now look at a marriage where the man is the head, and the woman takes the position as mediator between child and father. Think about it. Whenever you wanted something from your father, who did you go to? That's right, your mother! In the same way, Jesus makes intercession for us. An exchange between Jesus and God the Father always produces fruit, as reflected by the children.

God wants marriage to be a situation of practicing and reflecting oneness. "And the two are united into one" (Genesis 2:24 NLT; see also Matthew 19:4). This is the mandate of heaven. Of God Himself, who "worketh all things after the counsel of his own will: that we should be to the praise of his glory..." (Ephesians 1:11-12 KJV). No wonder they always agree! They've settled on a goal—the accomplishment of God's will. In that light all conclusions are reached. There's no need to stop and ask the angels, "What do you think?" They know their goal and what they want to accomplish on earth as well as in heaven. No one knows it better than they themselves—Father, Son, and Holy Spirit.

This is how it should work in marriage. You should know where you're going. The two of you should have a unified vision of your life together. If you do this, you'll eliminate the need for outside counsel and bad advice from friends who haven't the foggiest notion of God's goals and purposes for your lives as a couple. It is amazing to me how the very character of God is so deeply ingrained in our spirits, whether we acknowledge Him or not. Have you ever noticed how much men hate it when you discuss your personal business with a friend? That is the very heart of God! He counsels with Himself, and so do men. I am not ruling out counseling as an option if the two of you run into problems, but what I *am* saying is that you need to treat your heart-to-heart conversations as confidential and precious. Other people in your life might not feel the same need to treat your business as a thing of value. So guard your relationship as you would your own heart. This thing is between you and your man—no one else.

Marriage is the theater of heaven where our lives play out the scenario of God's foreordained purpose—complete oneness. Marriage exists to bring honor to God. As we bring honor to God, we are crowned with honor ourselves. That's the complete circle. People should look at your marriage and say, "Wow, there's something different about you two. What is it that makes your marriage so special?" That's your cue to say, "It's the Lord who makes the difference." People in the world will want what you have when you decide to make oneness the goal of your marriage. Oneness will give birth to a rich testimony that brings honor to God and joy, peace, and fulfillment to you.

So marriage is less about you than you thought, hmm? This is a good thing! You'll be less apt to get in the way of what God wants to accomplish through the two of you. You'll have to keep referring to His blueprint in order to complete His design. This is why it's so important not to get ahead of Him in the process of getting a mate. There are two ways to be married—in the will of God, and out of the will of God. One leads to endless rewards, the other to certain defeat and despair.

What is the best way to end up in the center of God's will? Walk with open hands and an obedient heart. This is what following all of the aforementioned principles will do for you. Only a *Principles* woman who is sold out to Christ and experiencing the joy of her salvation will be able to do this. So even though the Pleasure Principle should have been the first principle, I deliberately put it last so that it would be at the top of your mind when you finished reading this book.

It's of paramount importance to know and understand that marriage was created to honor God, not satisfy you. Your satisfaction just happens to be a wonderful and automatic by-product when it's done God's way. So live to glorify God in your marriage, "That ye may with one mind and one mouth glorify God, even the Father of our Lord Jesus Christ" (Romans 15:6 KJV). "Therefore glorify God in your body, and in your spirit, which are God's" (1 Corinthians 6:20 KJV). That is the bottom line—all we are and all that we have belong to God, including our marriage. Settle this in your heart as you prepare yourself for the one who God will send. I guarantee that you will judge all potential mates in a different light! You'll have to, because everything in your world will be bound to look different once you see it through the eyes of God's vision for your life. So get excited—the possibilities are endless!

Prayer

Dear Heavenly Father, I lay all of my expectations for marriage at Your feet and I choose to leave them there. Please rearrange the priorities of my heart to match Your agenda for my life. Give me a revelation of Your vision and purpose for marriage. Superimpose Your design for marriage over my own selfish longings and rationalizations. Open my ears to hear Your direction in relationship to my husband. Help me to be a doer of those things You ask of me. Lord, prepare me completely to be a vessel of blessing and inspiration to my husband. Let everything I do in my relationship with the one You choose to bless me with bring glory and honor to You, in Jesus' Name. Amen.

The Final Principle

*F*inally, my sisters, embrace life for all it's worth! Learn to fall in love with life itself. Live life to the fullest, drain all you can out of it, and watch your joy level rise to new heights. This is your time to celebrate you! Celebrate God! Celebrate the brilliant future that He is planning for you. Settle your heart now to be all that He has called you to be in the relationship that He is going to bless you with. And by all means, don't feel that after you arrive at the threshold of marriage you can now relax and let your act get raggedy.

I heard a wise woman once say, "Whatever you did to get that man, you'd better continue to do to keep him." There will always be someone younger than you and cuter than you waiting for the opportunity to take care of what you neglect. Cultivate godly habits now that you can continue to perfect throughout your marriage to increase you and your mate's happiness. This is why it's so important to become a whole, fulfilled person *first* so that you naturally do the principles I've laid out for you. That's much easier than pretending to be someone that you're not!

Nothing should change after the "I do's" are said. Consistency breeds security in relationships. That's why the Word of God says that with Him there is no "variableness, neither shadow of turning" (James 1:17 KJV). God remains the same. He never changes. You can rely on Him to stick to His word. He doesn't get convenient amnesia and decide to change the rules in the middle of your relationship with Him. As you know, you'll only be able to keep up an act for so long, but you will always be you.

So be yourself, but strive to walk in the spirit. Allow the Holy Spirit to control your life, and he will produce fruit in you that will make it easy to follow *The Principles*. Before you know it, love, joy, peace, patience, kindness, goodness, faithfulness, gentleness, and self-control will be just naturally oozing out of your pores!

The bottom line to the success of this whole relationship thing is practicing self-control and yielding to God's program so that He can honor and crown you with a healthy and blessed union. One where you will be able to rest secure in knowing that you are a precious addition to your man's life. Every area of life includes disciplines that must be followed in order to ensure success. Keep in mind that these principles are for your own self-preservation, emotional wholeness, and victory. Overeating causes weight gain, overspending causes financial difficulty, and not yielding to God's design for love will cause you to do things that will get you what you think you want momentarily, but which have no lasting reward.

As tempting as some situations may be, recognize them as the deception of sin. They may be pleasurable for a season, but you'll reap a harvest of regrets later. Keep your eye on the goal of marriage, and don't settle for a temporary fix. "Looking unto Jesus the author and finisher of our faith; who for the joy that was set before him, endured the cross, despising the shame, and is set down at the right hand of the throne of God" (Hebrews 12:2 KJV). Even Jesus had to endure some things, going through moments He would rather have avoided, in order to get what He wanted. How much more will we have to decide to sacrifice some things in order to stay on course and claim the ultimate prize? As they say in the world, *no pain, no gain*. In those weak moments, feel free to call on the Lord, and He will strengthen you to do the right thing. Remember, "Those who belong to Christ Jesus have nailed the passions and desires of their sinful nature to his cross and crucified them there. If we are living now by the Holy Spirit, let us follow the Holy Spirit's leading in every part of our lives" (Galatians 5:24-25 NLT).

So take courage—hold out for the prize. Count yourself as a valuable commodity. But don't forget, so is your mate! If you want him to continue to be romantic, you must continue to inspire him. If you want him to continue to think you are the most gorgeous creature on the face of the earth, you have to keep yourself together, inside and out. Don't fall down on the job just because you've signed a contract and have begun to experience the benefits. Life will always only be as good as you make it, and that sure is true with marriage.

The bottom line is that marriage is work, and if you don't do the work, you won't reap the rewards. Always examine yourself first before accusing. Speak the truth in love. Understand that your home will be the greatest mission field you'll ever inhabit. Your marriage is your primary ministry. If you are in church ministry, force yourself to find a place of balance. Don't let the headiness of being needed by others cause you to neglect the needs of your own household. God will not be pleased. Remember, Jesus preferred the heart of Mary over the busyness of Martha, even though her intentions were good. He said that Mary had chosen the better part— sitting at His feet. Don't make your husband choose between releasing you to God's service and attending to his needs. It will never be a comfortable choice for him, and he will ultimately resent you for putting him in that position. It can also affect his attitude toward God negatively.

The church is God's bride. He is well able to shower the body with His love, and He doesn't need your assistance in that area. He merely asks you to feed His sheep. No one—animal or human— feeds continuously; we all have appointed feeding times. So love your mate, and feed the sheep. Otherwise you're operating out of order. I have a friend who has a thriving ministry, but she has disciplined herself to only accept so many speaking engagements per month. And if her husband has an engagement, she defers to his schedule and forfeits her plans. Her reasoning for this is simple but profound: "I refuse to be out saving the world while allowing my household to go to hell." Think about it!

Too many ministers have problems in their marriages. This is not glorifying to God. It is a stumbling block to the church and a rock of offense to the world. Too many ministers' children are angry with the church because they feel they have been neglected by their parents and displaced by God. This is not God's design, and the severe consequences for these actions affect the body of Christ as a whole. This is not a new problem. Throughout the Bible, the children of the mighty prophets were wayward. So much so, that the children of Israel asked for a king because they did not want Samuel's children to judge them. Perhaps this is why God made "ruling his own house well" (1 Timothy 3:4) one of the requirements for the leaders of the church. It goes on in verse 5: "For if a man know not how to rule his own house, how shall he take care of the church of God?" (KJV). Can I get a witness?

Never rely on the understanding of your husband as you put all your energy into ministering to the masses. Yes, he is supposed to be a "man of God," but the operative word in this phrase is *man.* He is a *man* before he is a *man of God.* His flesh still has needs. No one walks in the spirit twenty-four hours a day. God knows this! He has instructed us not to neglect our husbands in the area of intimate ministry because such neglect will give place to the devil. "The husband should not deprive his wife of sexual intimacy, which is her right as a married woman, nor should the wife deprive her husband. The wife gives authority over her body to her husband and the husband also gives authority over his body to his wife. So do not deprive each other of sexual relations. The only exception to this rule would be the agreement of both husband and wife to refrain from sexual intimacy for a limited time so they can give themselves more completely to prayer. Afterward they should come together again so that Satan won't be able to tempt them because of their lack of self-control" (1 Corinthians 7:3-5 NLT). Now that's the Bible talking, not Michelle. So listen up! Do not disobey these instructions and then scratch your head, get mad at your mate, and later wonder what happened. You now know better!

If you have a problem fulfilling the ministry of your marriage in the bedroom and beyond, simply remember why you wanted to be married in the first place. This is one area where I do not recommend, "Forgetting those things which are behind..." I think it would do you well to remember your heart's cry as a single and continually rejoice and partake of the blessing that you have been given. To do anything less is a slap in the face of God.

So embrace your life now and live it to the fullest. And when he who will come, comes, fulfill your calling in the marriage arena with as much gusto as you imagined doing so as a single. Continue to be a *Principles* woman of excellence and virtue. In this, God, your husband, and your children will be well-pleased and arise and call you blessed.

Prayer

Dear Heavenly Father, as You prepare me to be the type of mate that You have called me to be, never let me take the blessing You give for granted. Help me to honor my commitment joyfully each and every day. Order my footsteps and my thoughts. Give me a fresh outpouring of love for my mate daily. Help me to do him good and not evil all his days. Help me to be sensitive to the needs of my household and do all things in balance. Let my marriage be a union and a ministry that brings glory to You, in Jesus' Name. Amen.

The Principle Recap

Now those of you '90s women who are still smarting from the last few chapters, remember—being politically correct only makes you popular with people who can't do anything about the areas of your life that really matter to you. However, being *spiritually* correct will grant you heaven on earth in the form of righteousness, peace, and joy in the Holy Ghost. That spills over into your life in the physical realm as well. Remember, when you do things God's way, blessings are guaranteed because He always honors His word. Become diligent in praying for your husband today even though you cannot see him. Do your prep work in the spirit now to prepare yourself for him and to prepare him for you. He needs your prayers wherever he is. After all, he's somewhere asking God where you are! So get ready, girl, and get these principles under your belt, safe and secure in your spirit:

1. *Take Art Appreciation*

2. *Stop playing with Daisies!*

3. *Get a Life!*

4. *Mind Your Own Business*

5. *Develop Good Shopping Skills*

6. *Avoid the Mission Field*

7. *Protect Your Jewels*

8. *Use a Lot of Seasoning*

9. *Know How to Take Advice*

10. *Learn How to Dress*

11. *Master the Art of Cooking*

12. *Know How to Sow*

13. *Get into Gardening*

14. *Learn How to Dance*

15. *Know Who Loves Ya, Baby!*

16. *Know What You Want*

17. *Know If He's the One*

18. *Master the Art of Housekeeping*

19. *Understand the Pleasure Principle*

20. *Practice the Final Principle*

21. *Remember the Principles and Don't Compromise!*

In the world, you'll always find an exception to the Principles. However, even if God chooses to do a "new thing" it won't be in violation of His written word. So if you feel "led" to do something that your responsible Christian friends are saying is not scriptural, stop rationalizing and justifying, and examine the spirits to see which one you were influenced by. Remember, you are capable of hearing three voices—the voice of God, the voice of Satan, and the voice of your own desires. Three very strong spirits! And believe me, God will not attempt to shout above you and the devil. He quietly says what He has to say and moves on. After all, He wrote the Book. What else do you need?

So follow the Principles. Ignore the world's rules. What you decide can make or break your heart. And the choice is entirely up to you. God won't force you, but perhaps your desire for getting past where you are now will inspire you to repent of your past self-defeating habits and get on with the business of getting the victory. So decide to be a well-kept woman kept by God, kept by your own sense of personal value. After all, you've got Principles.

Recommended Reading

31 Secrets of an Unforgettable Woman by Mike Murdoch

Knight in Shining Armor by P. B. Wilson (Harvest House)

The Master's Degree by Frank & P. B. Wilson (Harvest House)

Men Who Can't Love by Steven Carter & Julie Sokol (Berkley)

Women Men Love, Women Men Leave by Dr. Connell Cowan & Dr. Melvin Kinder (Signet)

SEX, LOVE or INFATUATION How Can I Really Know? by Ray E. Short (Augsburg)

God's Design for Christian Dating by Greg Laurie (Harvest House)

Finding Your Perfect Mate by H. Norman Wright (Harvest House)

Before You Say I Do by H. Norman Wright (Harvest House)

God Is a Match-maker by Derek Prince (Chosen)

The Mystery of Marriage by Mike Mason (Multnomah Books)

MAILING ADDRESS:
Michelle McKinney Hammond
c/o HeartWing Ministries
P.O. Box 11052
Chicago, IL 60611

Study Guide

Chapter One

All Rules Made to Be Broken? I Don't Think So, Girlfriend!

Scripture Passage: 1 Samuel 15:1-23

This story mirrors several times in my own life when I chose to do things my way in the face of opposite instructions from the Lord. Like Saul, I had several good reasons to justify my actions when confronted by the Holy Spirit. Whether it was my own lack of trust in Him, impatience, peer pressure, the fear of looking foolish, or just good old willful stubbornness, I alone discovered that temporary pleasure wasn't worth the painful consequences of my actions.

Key Phrase: *"Stubbornness is as iniquity and idolatry"* (verse 23 KJV).

1. Why is stubbornness sin?

2. Why is stubbornness compared to idolatry?

3. How does stubbornness keep us from progressing? (Psalm 66:18)

4. In the area of relationships, what self-defeating habits do you cling to with a vengeance? Why?

5. Are there habits (or persons) God has asked you to release that you still cling to? What (or who) are they?

6. What fears are linked to these habits?

7. What does the Word of God say about these habits?

8. What can God do about your situation?

9. What must you do first?

10. List five steps you will take to break your habit. Find a Scripture to stand on for each step.

Chapter Two

So Who Wrote the Rules Anyway?

Scripture Passage: Deuteronomy 30: 11-20

God graciously gives us the choice of doing things His way or our way. But we must be aware that our choice holds the potential for tremendous blessings or painful curses. Whether it be the work of our hands, our homes, or our relationships, there is a price to be paid for violating God's principles. We can breathe life or death into everything concerning us. The choice is ours.

Key Phrase: *"...I call on heaven and earth to witness the choice you make. Oh, that you would choose life..."* (verse 19 NLT).

1. Why does God leave the choice of obedience up to us?

2. What are blessings? What are curses?

3. How does this passage apply to your love life?

4. According to these verses, what would happen to your relationship if you were obedient to God's Word? If you were disobedient?

5. What are the gods in your heart in the areas of romance and marriage?

6. How have you previously violated God's Word in your former relationships? What were the results?

7. What does God's Word say about these violations?

8. What do you need to do to get back on track?

9. What Scripture can you stand on for strength? Can a friend hold you accountable?

10. Set a goal with God, and write down realistic steps to restoration.

Chapter Three

A Woman of Spiritual Principle

Scripture Passages: Genesis 17:1-22; 32:22-32

It is essential for each one of us to have a face-to-face encounter with God. We must see Him as He is in order to see ourselves. As we see ourselves as He sees us, the very complexion of our lives is bound to change. An encounter with our Heavenly Father always has a way of transforming us inwardly and changing our names, the very confession of our lives.

Key Phrase: "...*Your name will no longer be Jacob because you have struggled with both God and men and have won*" (32:28 NLT).

1. What has been the biggest area of struggle you've had in relationships?

2. Have you struggled with God in the same area?

3. What is the root of your struggle?

4. Do you know who you are? Who are you according to yourself? According to God?

5. What does God say you deserve?

6. Have you been living beneath your privilege in relationships? In what areas?

7. What habits or mindsets cause you live beneath your God-ordained privilege?

8. What promises has God made to you concerning your life?

9. What are you expecting from God?

10. What would you like your name to be changed to?

11. What covenant are you willing to make with God to see His promises come to fruition in your life?

Principle #1

Take Art Appreciation

Scripture Passages: Psalm 139:13-18; Genesis 1:27,31

Sometimes it is not a conscious thought on our part that God carefully formed us. We must be ever cognizant that none of us were an accident. We were foreordained to be here. Every detail of our existence was planned out in great detail, including the way we look! Oh, if we could only have the eyes of God to see the beauty that He sees in us!

Key Phrase: *"Then God looked over all he had made, and he saw that it was excellent in every way"* (Genesis 1:31 NLT).

1. What is true beauty according to the world? According to God?

2. Which standard should you uphold? Why?

3. How has the world's standard of beauty changed through the years?

4. Has God's standard of beauty changed? Is His standard easier or harder to live up to than the world's standard? Why?

5. Where does the real work begin in order to cultivate real beauty?

6. Reflect on someone you know and consider beautiful. What makes this person beautiful to you?

7. What are your best inner attributes? Your best outer attributes?

8. What would you like to change? Why?

9. Would God agree with your observation? Based on which Scripture?

10. What steps can you take to improve your areas that need beautifying? Which Scriptures will you stand on?

Principle #2

Stop Playing with Daisies

Scripture Passages: 1 Corinthians 13:4-7; 1 John 4:7-20

The world has given us so many false images of what true love looks and feels like that our expectations have taken a nose-dive. But God has set a standard for love by His own actions. It is His desire for us to experience love to the fullest degree in order for us to pour out as we have received.

Key Phrase: *"God showed how much he loved us by sending his only Son into the world so that we might have eternal life through him. This is real love. It is not that we loved God, but that he loved us and sent his Son as a sacrifice to take away our sins"* (1 John 4:9-10 NLT).

1. What is the ultimate expression of love?

2. Who makes you feel the most loved? Why?

3. What did you do to gain that person's attention and love? Why does he or she love you?

4. What happened in your last relationship to make you feel unloved?

5. How did you respond to this treatment? Was this just one instance, or is it a cycle?

6. Do you find yourself striving to win love in relationships? Why?

7. What kind of things do you do? What is the reaction to your actions?

8. Are your actions guided by God's Word or your own ideas?

9. How does God say you deserve to be loved? How are you to love others?

10. What new standards for love will you set for your life?

11. What blind spots and problem areas will you make note to avoid?

Principle #3

Get a Life!

Scripture Passage: Philippians 3:12-14

Before you existed, or were even a thought in the heart of your parents, you existed in the heart of God. You are the personification of something that He wanted to do. As you find the center of God's will for your life, you will discover the void you felt for so long was really your spirit's longing to line up with the purpose for which it had been created.

Key Phrase: "*I press on, that I may lay hold of that for which Christ Jesus has also laid hold of me*" (verse 12 NKJV).

1. What are you striving to achieve?

2. What is your God-ordained purpose? Are you operating within your calling? If yes, how? If no, why not?

3. What secret desire has been in your heart that you've not pursued?

4. What is the gift that others appreciate in you?

5. How can you channel this gift into a productive kingdom tool?

6. What is the burden of your heart for others?

7. How can this be converted into a ministry?

8. What is keeping you from stepping out?

9. What do you need in order to start putting your dream into action?

10. List five things that you will do to begin fulfilling your dream. Find someone to hold you accountable.

Principle #4

Mind Your Own Business

Scripture Passage: Psalm 37:3-6

There is much to be said for leaving the driving in our lives to God. It keeps us out of harm's way. That is what is so beautiful about the imagery of the sheep and the shepherd. Sheep just graze and chill, while the shepherd leads them to safe pastures and watches over them, keeping them safe from all hurt, harm, and danger. What a wonderful life! We have the same privilege. We fall prey to the same danger as the sheep who decides to wander off on its own in search of undiscovered pasture. Some sheep have been known to eat their way right off a cliff, and so it is with us when we don't look up and decide to go our own way instead.

Key Phrase: *"Then you will live safely in the land and prosper"* (verse 3 NLT).

1. What happens when you decide to leave God's safety zone?

2. What usually prompts you to do this?

3. What happens afterward?

4. Has this become a recurring pattern in your life?

5. How can you break the cycle?

6. Do you trust the Lord with this area of your life? If yes, how? If no, why not?

7. Are you willing to completely surrender this desire to the Lord?

8. What fears do you have in this area? What do you think the Lord will do if you release your longing for love to Him?

9. What does "Delight yourself in the Lord" mean to you? How did Mary delight herself in God? What cues can you take from her?

10. Do you believe God is interested in your love life?

11. List five ways you can redirect your focus toward God.

Principle #5

Develop Good Shopping Skills

Scripture Passage: Psalm 119:34-37,65-68

How can you get to know someone without making a huge emotional investment? How do you avoid making the mistakes you've made in the past? The world has its own solution for solidifying relationships—it pursues them without making realistic assessments of one another's character and finds itself wondering in dismay why the marriage didn't work later. We can choose to go the way of the world, or we can allow God to lead us to love.

Key Phrase: *"Turn my eyes from worthless things, and give me life through your word"* (verse 37 NLT).

1. Evaluate past dating experiences you've had. What was accomplished?

2. What are your expectations when you go on a date?

3. Do you believe the real person is revealed during a date?

4. How do you get to see the real person?

5. What does God have to do with the dating experience?

6. How can you utilize His help to see the true character of the person you're interested in?

7. What are some other ways you can get to know people?

8. What situations reveal the true character of a person to you?

9. What should be the real goal of your encounters with people? How do you accomplish this?

10. List five creative ways to get to know a person.

Principle #6

Avoid the Mission Field

Scripture Passage: 2 Corinthians 6:13–7:1

As the saying goes, "What's good to you, isn't always good for you." Things aren't always what they seem. The enemy specializes in coming disguised as an angel of light. He will bless you in order to bind you. Some pain in life is unavoidable, but some is downright unnecessary. This is where maturity usurps the demands of fleshly desires.

Key Phrase: *"Because we have these promises, dear friends, let us cleanse ourselves from everything that can defile our body or spirit"* (7:1 NLT).

1. What causes you to consider settling for less than God's best?

2. How do men in the world react to your standards for living?

3. What areas of your life can be affected by an unbelieving mate?

4. How easy is it to maintain your walk with the Lord when you are intimately involved with unbelievers?

5. What are your weak areas that are susceptible when in the company of unbelievers?

6. What traits are you looking for in a mate?

7. Are all of these traits found in unbelievers? Which ones are present? Which ones are missing? Which are most important?

8. Write a statement of recommitment to trust God to deliver His best for you.

Principle #7

Protect Your Jewels

Scripture Passages: Matthew 6:21; Luke 2:19; Proverbs 4:23

There is nothing more comforting than knowing you have a safe place to hide your heart. We all long to have a confidante with whom we can share our deepest secrets, longings, and hurts. But it's difficult to discern who we can turn to with this information. Who can we trust to protect our hearts and shield us from further pain? There is only One who deserves that level of confidence, and that is God Himself.

Key Phrase: *"Guard your heart, for it affects everything you do"* (Proverbs 4:23 NLT).

1. When you hurt, who do you turn to?

2. Who is ultimately able to deal with the things that affect your heart?

3. What are the steps to healing that you can take?

4. What are the self-defeating habits or characteristics that you have disclosed in past relationships?

5. Why did you feel a need to share these things with the man in your life?

6. What negative or positive feedback did you receive from him?

7. How did it affect your relationship? Were these conversations ever revisited? In what light?

8. What areas do you feel were necessary to be shared? Which can be categorized as venting?

9. What were you looking for as a reaction to the things you shared?

10. Write the things that have wounded you and keep resurfacing in your heart, and give them to the Lord. Covenant with Him for a complete healing.

Principle #8

Use a Bot of Seasoning

Scripture Passage: James 3:5

Have you ever been around someone who never had anything good to say? Or been influenced negatively by words of doubt spoken to you? Have you ever decided that you didn't want to be around someone because the words of their mouth were too offensive? Too harsh? Too much of a downer? We are all drawn to, or repelled by, certain people based on the things that proceed out of their mouths. Consider how the words of your mouth affect your loved ones.

Key Phrase: *"The tongue is a small thing, but what enormous damage it can do"* (NLT).

1. Have you ever been a victim of words? What was said? How did the words affect you?

2. Have you ever been inspired by words? What was said? How did it affect you?

3. What effect would you like to have on your loved ones? How will your selection of words prove helpful in accomplishing this goal?

4. What are your weak spots where you fall into conversation that is not edifying?

5. What safeguards can you set for yourself to keep this from happening?

6. How do you speak the truth in love?

7. What should be your motivation for speaking the truth?

8. What are some of the ways you can check your motivation for the things you say?

9. What affects your conversation?

10. Make a list of five steps you can take to weed out the negatives in your conversation.

Principle #9

Know How to Take Advice

Scripture Passages: Proverbs 2:12; 4:6-7; 27:6,9

I am of the opinion that we should find someone who is doing what we would like to do and glean as much advice from that person as we can. We know that opinions are like noses—everyone has one, but how many of them are truly desirable? Don't allow pride to make you walk in ignorance. When in doubt, ask someone qualified to answer the question. Hold yourself accountable to someone who can speak the truth in love to you and reap the rewards of good advice.

Key Phrase: *"Getting wisdom is the most important thing you can do! And whatever else you do, get good judgment"* (4:7 NLT).

1. What did your refusal to listen to advice cost you in the past?

2. What was your reason for not listening at the time?

3. What was a situation where good counsel saved you?

4. What was your reason for listening?

5. Are you able to be objective about circumstances in your life, especially in the arena of love?

6. What type of counsel are you seeking for your life? Is there anyone available in your circle to give you that type of counsel?

7. What advice would you give to a friend who was in your circumstance?

8. What areas do you struggle with in terms of keeping yourself honest and seeing things as they really are?

9. What are you hoping to avoid by not acknowledging the truth?

10. Select a friend to hold you accountable in your relationships. Make a list of the areas where you need help.

Principle #10

Learn How to Dress

Scripture Passages: Isaiah 52:7, 1 Peter 3:3-5; 1 Timothy 2:10

The world puts such harsh requirements on us to live up to the standard of beauty that's been set. I am relieved, however, that most people who have any sense of depth can see past it. "Pretty is as pretty does," is a saying that I still find quite relevant. The people who I find beautiful in my life are the ones who lift my spirits, and put a smile on my lips and laughter in my heart. They are truly a sight for sore eyes. Let's look again at this thing called beauty!

Key Phrase: *"You should be known for the beauty that comes from within, the unfading beauty of a gentle and quiet spirit, which is so precious to God"* (1 Peter 3:4).

1. List a few people who you find outstanding in outer beauty. Why?

2. List their inner qualities. Do they match the outer shell?

3. List a few people who are not necessarily beautiful according to the world's standards, but who you find attractive. What do you think is attractive about them?

4. List their inner qualities. Which makes the stronger impression on your feelings toward them—inner or outer? Why?

5. What are your most outstanding inward features? Outward features?

6. Why do people like you?

7. Why do you like you? If you don't like you, why not?

8. What areas of your spirit need a day at the spa with Jesus?

9. What parts of you do you feel others deserve more of? Why?

10. What part of your character do you think glorifies God the most? Why?

11. Outline a beauty regime for your spirit.

Principle #11

Master the Art of Cooking

Scripture Passages: Romans 6:12,13; 8:13; 1 Corinthians 6:18-20

Sometimes I think we forget that our bodies no longer belong to us. We forget that they've been purchased and are considered a precious treasure. We are no longer at liberty to cast them about at will. Once, while discussing the ridiculously expensive price of an outfit, a friend told me, "I simply cannot spend God's money that way." Do you stop to think what you are doing to God's body when you ignore His Word?

Key Phrase: *"You were bought at a price. Therefore honor God with your body"* (1 Corinthians 6:20 NIV).

1. What are your areas of vulnerability in the area of sexuality?

2. What precautions can you take to safeguard your purity?

3. How much does your thought life figure into the equation? In what way?

4. What steps can you take to quiet the screaming of your flesh?

5. What effect has sex had on your past relationships? Are there any cycles that occur?

6. In what way does sex dilute your discernment in relationships?

7. Do you feel you have any soul ties from past relationships? What are the effects? Pray and ask God to sever them.

8. What are steps you can take toward putting a lid on your thought life? Your desires?

9. How can you become a living sacrifice?

10. What does your body mean to you? To God?

Principle #12

Know How to Sow

Scripture Passages: Psalm 126:5; Hosea 10:12; 2 Corinthians 9:6;
Galatians 6:8-9

Even when someone's not saved, the law of the spirit operates.
Even the unrighteous benefit from the law of giving. They are uti-
lizing the law of giving and reaping a harvest from it. Perhaps you
don't have a lot of money, but you do have a lot of love to give.
Across the board, the same rule applies.

Key Phrase: *"Sow for yourselves righteousness, reap the fruit of
unfailing love"* (Hosea 10:12 NIV).

1. In what areas of your life have you been selfish or self-
   absorbed?

2. Where do you feel a large void in your life? How can you fill
   it?

3. What gifts do you have that can be enjoyed by others? Are
   you sharing them generously?

4. What are the hindrances to your ability to give? Physically?
   Emotionally? Spiritually?

5. What would you like to receive from others? Are you giving what you would like to receive?

6. How much free time do you have? What are you doing with it?

7. Is most of your free time spent on yourself or on others?

8. How and why does self-absorption lead to feelings of hopelessness?

9. What are some steps you can take to lead you out of self?

10. How can you actively share your gifts and your love with others?

Principle #13

Get into Gardening

Scripture Passages: Jeremiah 24:3-7; Proverbs 1:31; 12:14;
   Ezekiel 17:23; Colossians 1:10; Galatians 5:22

Sometimes we wonder why we are where we are. But God has carved the path beneath our steps to bring us to a predetermined place. To work something out in us. To bring us to the end of ourselves and the beginning of where He wants us to be. When a rosebud is being pruned it looks pretty miserable, but, oh, the blossoms that will spring forth. Wait until you see the new you!

Key Phrase: "*I have sent them into captivity for their own good*"
   (Jeremiah 24:5 NLT).

1. What old weeds do you need to dig up out of the garden of your heart?

2. Which of your attitudes and beliefs are not bearing godly fruit? Why do you allow them to remain?

3. What would you like to see growing in your heart? What is stopping that from happening?

4. How can you keep the weeds from returning? Which mistakes should you not repeat?

5. What type of things are fertilizer for lush fruit in your life?

6. What does the fruit of your life say to others about your frame of mind? Your walk with Christ?

7. If you could be a fruit, which one would you be? Why?

8. Does your life resemble the fruit you just named? If yes, in what way? If no, why not?

9. What is hindering the fruit from coming forth in your life freely? What can be done to correct this?

10. List five gardening techniques you plan to use on your heart in order to become a garden bearing lush fruit.

Principle #14

Learn How to Dance

Scripture Passages: Romans 15:3-8; 1 Peter 3:6; Ephesians 5:21-24

Our submission to Christ will only be seen in the light of how we submit to one another. Therefore, how we submit to one another is one of our strongest witnesses to the world. In the submission equation, who is most important? Ourselves, or our reflection of Christ in us?

Key Phrase: *"For even Christ did not please Himself"* (Romans 15:3 NKJV).

1. What are your feelings about submission? Why?

2. What does God have to say about the way you feel?

3. What happens when two people try to walk through a door at the same time? How can this apply to your relationship?

4. Who gives the ultimate portrayal of submission in the Bible? Did submission diminish this person's status in any way?

5. How is submission liberating?

6. What do you gain from submitting?

7. How do you relate to your boss in the area of submission? Outwardly? Inwardly?

8. How does resisting the authority of others affect your relationships? Your job? Your spiritual well-being?

9. List the ways in which submission is good for you.

10. Make note of the situations in your life that require a change of attitude in the area of submission. Make a list of steps you can take in order to get back on track.

Principal #15

Know Who Loves Ya, Baby!

Scripture Passages: Song of Songs 5:6-7; Proverbs 18:22

How many times have we set ourselves up for rejection and failed to see our own responsibility in the fallout? Beneath the umbrella of God's Word, provision has been made to keep us safe from the rain of unnecessary pain. Yet from time to time we wander out from under its protection, fascinated by mirages that appear in the distance. True maturity is when we are able to stay put and allow others to join us beneath the shelter of God's Word.

Key Phrase: *"The watchmen found me as they were making their rounds; they struck and wounded me"* (Song of Songs 5:7 NLT).

1. Why do you feel the need to make things happen in the realm of relationships?

2. Do you consider yourself desirable? If yes, why? If no, why not?

3. What types of things do you do in order to gain attention from the opposite sex? How do your actions line up with Scripture?

4. Do your attention-getting techniques work long-term? Where do you see possible problems with your strategy?

5. What worldly approaches do you find yourself adopting in the pursuit of relationships?

6. What steps can you take to make yourself actively passive in the initial stages of interest?

7. Find a Scripture to meditate on that addresses your own self-worth. How can you personalize this Scripture?

8. List your attributes that will make you a prize catch for someone. If you can't think of any, then you know what you need to work on before attempting another relationship!

9. Write down what God thinks of you, and compare it to what *you* think of you.

10. Consider going on a "man fast" for a period of six months. Keep a journal of the things you learn about yourself during this time.

Principle #16

Know What You Want

Scripture Passages: Genesis 2:18; 1 Corinthians 11:7-12

The decade of liberation has done more to put men and women in bondage than ever before. The freedoms supposedly gained seem to be enjoyed alone more and more. In the wake of fighting for equality, everyone has become quite confused about their role in the play of life and love. What God said from the beginning still stands. The sooner we return to our spiritual roots as women, the more joyful and open to love we will find ourselves.

Key Phrase: *"And the* LORD *God said, "It is not good for the man to be alone. I will make a companion who will help him"* (Genesis 2:18 NLT).

1. What is your perception of a wife's role?

2. What are your qualifications for being a wife?

3. Make a list of God's qualifications for being a wife. Do you measure up? In what areas do you need work?

4. Where are your areas of conflict between what the world says and what God says about the role of a wife?

5. What is the benefit of complete autonomy?

6. What is the benefit of a thriving partnership?

7. Does it matter who gets the credit if great rewards are gained for both husband and wife to enjoy equally? If yes, why? If no, why not?

8. Why is it important for you to follow God's design for a wife?

9. How can your actions affect your husband? Your children?

10. Make an honest evaluation of your qualifications and attitudes about the role of wife. Make a list of the areas where you need God to help you understand and submit to His design.

Principle #17

Know If He's the One

Scripture Passages: 1 Peter 3:7; Ephesians 5:21-23

The man in your life has been called to the priesthood. This means he is called to pour out his life, wash your soul, and sustain you and your children spiritually, emotionally, and physically. Are you checking out the men you meet in light of that fact? I challenge you to dig a little deeper into the character of the man who you are considering.

Key Phrase: *"Husbands must love your wives with the same love Christ showed the church"* (Ephesians 5:25 NLT).

1. Write down what you desire in a mate. How many things on your list are inner qualities? Which ones are included in the list that Paul gives to Timothy?

2. What usually attracts you to a man? Are any of these lasting attributes?

3. Which of the things that caused the initial attraction are things that give you clues to his character long-term?

4. Which qualities will you need your husband to exhibit outside of the bedroom? Inside of the bedroom? Where will most of your time be spent?

5. Do you take the time to measure the character of the man you are attracted to? How many things in him do you plan to change?

6. Are you open to allowing God to change your concept of what your mate should be like?

7. Do you consider if you can joyfully assist and complement this man? Do you have common goals and interests?

8. Do you take the time to see if he is a man with a vision and an understanding of his call as a husband?

9. What is his relationship with God like? Does he open up things to you that you failed to see about God before? Who is the spiritual leader in the relationship?

10. Now make a new list of what you should be looking for, according to God. Surrender your wants (your earlier list) to God.

Principle #18

Master the Art of Housekeeping

Scripture Passages: Romans 12:1-2; 1 Peter 1:13-20; Isaiah 54:1-8; Psalm 113:9

Sometimes a blessing is not found in the place where we look for it, but in the very thing from which we turn away. This year I've been blessed with the responsibility of being the legal guardian for my cousin's two teenage girls from Africa as they attend school in the States. It has been a rich and fulfilling experience for me, one that filled an empty place in my life beyond my imagination. It has also been very sobering. Motherhood is a tremendous and miraculous blessing, but it is also bears awesome responsibilities. It truly made me take off the rose-colored glasses and realize the fact that the things we think we crave require our willingness to commit ourselves to hard work. I've also realized how my singleness is a blessing to someone who needs my availability. Therefore this has caused me to purpose in my heart to wait for the appointed day and to maintain holiness as I wait for the fulfillment of my personal dreams.

Key Phrase: "He maketh the barren woman to keep house, and to be a joyful mother of children" (Psalm 113:9 KJV).

1. How has compromising God's principles cost you in the past?

2. What do you determine your value to be?

3. How do you get others to treat you as you deserve to be treated?

4. How does God want you to keep your vessel?

5. How does doing things God's way profit you?

6. How can you make sure your children enjoy the full richness of God's blessings in their lives?

7. How can you prepare yourself to be a good mother?

8. What opportunities can you take advantage of now to prepare yourself for marriage and parenting?

9. What will you determine your stand to be as a *Principles* woman?

10. List five standards for yourself to uphold in your relationships with men. Ask a friend to hold you accountable.

The Pleasure Principle

Scripture Passage: Genesis 1:26-31

God's design for marriage and our role in marriage was perfect and to the benefit of both parties involved. Sin created an imbalance that we are still reeling from. Through the blood of Jesus and out of submission to the Word of God, we hold the awesome ability to cooperate with God and reap the benefits of obedience. Let's do this thing right! For us there is no excuse. We've been given all the tools.

Key Phrase: *"Then God looked over all he had made, and he saw that it was excellent in every way"* (verse 31 NLT).

1. What has been your concept of what marriage should be like?

2. Think of a marriage that has been a good example to you. What were the attributes of the man and woman? What impressed you about their union?

3. Think of a marriage that has been a bad example to you. What were the attributes of the man and woman? What upset you the most about what was taking place between them?

4. How do you feel when you see a bad marriage? How does it affect your attitude toward God and Christians?

5. List five things that make a marriage successful.

6. Do you feel that children can save a marriage? Why or why not?

7. Name some of the things that put pressure on a marriage.

8. Who is the real enemy of marriage? How should difficult situations between a husband and wife be reconciled?

9. How can "irreconcilable differences" be resolved?

10. Write your goals for what you would like your marriage to reflect to others.

Other Good
Harvest House Reading

WHERE ARE YOU GOD?
By Michelle McKinney Hammond

In this refreshingly original devotional, Michelle McKinney Hammond focuses on well-known men and women of the Bible who spent transforming moments alone with their creator. From Mary's times of pondering to Thomas' times of doubting, *His Love Always Finds Me* prepares hearts to find God in solitude, in the midst of a crowd, and in the heart of the inner journey.

WHAT TO DO UNTIL LOVE FINDS YOU
By Michelle McKinney Hammond

Are you ready to be found? Are you ready to leave the single life behind? Through insightful and often humorous illustrations, *What to Do Until Love Finds You* gives you straight talk on the challenges and victories of that time of your life before "forever love."

THE POWER OF BEING A WOMAN
By Michelle McKinney Hammond

With boldness and grace, Michelle tosses political correctness and challenges women to celebrate their gender differences. Readers will delight in Michelle's refreshing point of view on the power of influence, manipulation pitfalls, and strength in vulnerability.

WHAT BECOMES OF THE BROKEN HEARTED
By Michelle McKinney Hammond

Assuring women of God's constant presence, Michelle guides them through the stages of recapturing joy. Helping readers evaluate their situations and turn to God for healing, Michelle also provides biblical tools for handling strong emotions.

KNIGHT IN SHINING ARMOR
By P.B. Wilson

Breaking the holding pattern faced by many women who are waiting for their life partners, Wilson helps them become complete as a single, so they can bring all of their resources into marriage with joyful and realistic expectations.

FINDING YOUR PERFECT MATE
By H. Norman Wright

Thoughtful words of wisdom and encouragement on one of life's most important turning points. Dynamic insights based on years of premarital counseling for people who seek God's guidance in finding a perfect lifetime companion.

BEFORE YOU SAY I DO
By H. Norman Wright and Wes Roberts

With over 500,000 copies sold, this guide is now revised and updated for the '90s. Couples will explore how to clarify role expectations, establish a healthy sexual relationship, handle finances, and acquire a solid understanding of how to develop a biblical relationship.